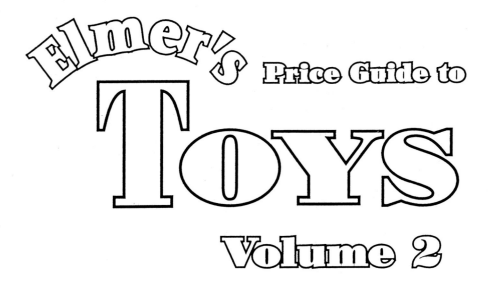

Elmer's Price Guide to TOYS

Volume 2

By
Elmer Duellman

ISBN#: 0-89538-046-3

Published by: L-W Book Sales
               P.O. Box 69
               Gas City, IN 46933
Please write for our free catalog.

Printed by IMAGE GRAPHICS, INC., Paducah, Kentucky

Table of Contents

Dedication

Thank you to my wife, Bernadette, my children, son-in-law, and daughters-in-law. A very special thank you to Rod Shrimpton for all the help in making this book possible.

Pricing Information

The values listed in this book should be used only as a guide. These prices will vary from one region of the country to another. All prices are also affected by the condition as well as the demand of the toy.

Neither the author nor the publisher assumes responsibility for any gains or losses that may be incurred as a result of consulting this guide.

Elmer Duellman: The Man Behind the Toys

Elmer was born and still lives in picturesque Fountain City, Wisconsin, a small city along the Mississippi River.

His passion for toy collecting comes from his childhood. Growing up in a family of eight children, there weren't many toys available for any of them to enjoy.

When he was nine, he started fixing bicycles, then Cushman scooters and motorcycles. At fifteen, Elmer graduated to buying and selling full-sized cars, 42 of them by age eighteen. All of his life has been centered around his family and automobiles.

In 1962 Elmer married his wife Bernadette. They have six children: Les, Rick, Brad, Melissa, Eric, and Amanda.

Elmer owned an automotive salvage yard for 30 years; worked at and/or owned a full-service gasoline station and used car dealership since 1951. He drag raced when he was younger and still owns the 1958 Chevrolet he drove. Elmer also drove dirt track stock cars successfully for a few years. Today, besides his hobby of collecting and displaying toys, he works at the gas station and car dealership.

Elmer's home and museum are located on top of Eagle Bluff in Fountain City, Wisconsin, the highest point along the Mississippi River. The spectacular view of the river valley accents his collection and museum. Elmer's museum is open to the public one weekend a month from April to October.

Elmer started collecting toys when he was 22 years old. He would purchase all of the toys at local auctions even though everyone else thought that he was crazy. He enjoys and owns all types of toys, from the 1800's to modern day collectibles. In his collection and museum you will find a wide variety of toys, antique cars, classic cars, muscle cars, motorcycles, pedal cars, sleds, wagons, scooters, and pedal tractors. The toy variety includes pressed steel, Buddy L, Lehmann, Tootsie Toys, Japanese tin, cast iron, and modern day plastic. Elmer particularly enjoys automotive toys, race cars, and motorcycles. A couple of the rarest pieces he owns are the Guntherman Gordon Bennett Racer and the Lehmann Boxer Toy, which are depicted within Elmer's Toys- Volume I.

The most interesting part of owning toys for Elmer is that the toy market is always changing. The prices reflect what people like and enjoy the most. Elmer has fun dealing with people from all over the world. The toy world is VERY large. Elmer thinks toy collecting is something in which everyone can participate. You can buy expensive or inexpensive toys and have lots of fun with it.

Elmer likes to share his collection and hopes you enjoy this book. This book is the second volume of Elmer's Toys. The first book has been very successful and has captivated many toy collectors of all ages.

Look, read and enjoy....

Miscellaneous Automobiles

Roadster, 15 1/4", wind-up, by
Structo, made in USA

Good	Excellent	Mint
$400	$750	$1300

Sedan, 14", wind-up, made in
Great Britain

Good	Excellent	Mint
$150	$200	$300

Mercedes Micro Racer, 4 1/2",
wind-up, by Schuco, made in
Germany

Good	Excellent	Mint
$50	$75	$100

Red Car Coupe, 7", wind-up,
by Slik Toys, made in USA

Good	Excellent	Mint
$90	$120	$165

Miscellaneous Automobiles

'57 Chevy Delco Shock Special, 12", wind-up, by Wen Mac, made in USA

Good	Excellent	Mint
$80	$130	$175

Crash Car, 7", wind-up, made in France

Good	Excellent	Mint
$50	$75	$100

Two Man Gordon Bennet Racer #12, 7 1/4", wind-up

Rare

Miscellaneous Automobiles

Chrysler Convertible, 13 3/4",
friction powered, made in
Germany

Good	Excellent	Mint
$400	**$675**	**$950**

Cadillac, 12 1/4", friction
powered, by Gama, made
in West Germany

Good	Excellent	Mint
$400	**$650**	**$875**

'65 Fairlane, 8 1/4", friction
powered, by NK Toys, made
in Korea

Good	Excellent	Mint
$50	**$80**	**$125**

Opel, 10 1/4", friction powered, by
Gama, made in West Germany

Good	Excellent	Mint
$100	**$250**	**$350**

Miscellaneous Automobiles

Cadillac, 12 1/4", friction powered, by Gama, made in West Germany

Good	Excellent	Mint
$400	**$650**	**$875**

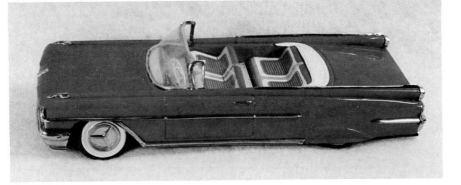

'59 Oldsmobile Custom Convertible, 13", friction powered, by Lennie, made in USA

Mint
$650

Airflow, 17", by Cor Cor, made in USA

Good	Excellent	Mint
$1200	**$1800**	-

Corvette, 12 1/2", by Hubley, made in USA

Good	Excellent	Mint
$150	**$250**	**$350**

Miscellaneous Automobiles

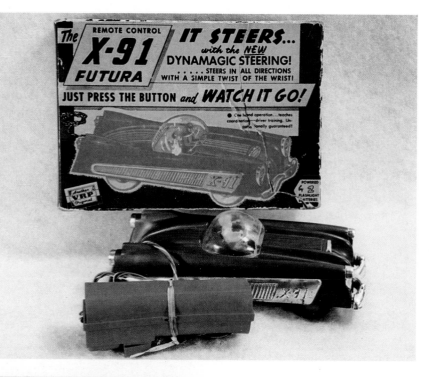

X-91 Futura, 8 3/4", remote
control, by VRP, Made in USA

Good	Excellent	Mint
$40	$100	$125

Thunderbird, 13 1/2", friction
powered, made in West Germany

Good	Excellent	Mint
$65	$110	$145

Hot Rod, 8", by Saunders,
made in USA

Good	Excellent	Mint
$30	$50	$90

Miscellaneous Automobiles

Testor Race Car #22, 12 1/2",
gas powered, made in USA

Good	Excellent	Mint
$75	**$100**	**$125**

Hot Rod, 10 1/2", gas
powered, by Renwal, made
in USA

Good	Excellent	Mint
$35	**$75**	**$135**

Mercedes Racer #18, 12 1/4",
by Marklin, made in Germany

Good	Excellent	Mint
-	-	**$400**

Miscellaneous Automobiles

Uhu Amphibian Auto, 8 1/4",
by Lehmann, made in Germany

Good	Excellent	Mint
$1000	**$1700**	**$2300**

'48 Hudson Bank, 7 1/2"

Good	Excellent	Mint
$50	**$80**	**$130**

'57 Dodge, 9 1/2", battery operated

Good	Excellent	Mint
$250	**$500**	**$700**

Miscellaneous Automobiles

'51 Chevy Bank, 8"

Good	Excellent	Mint
$60	**$100**	**$150**

Mystery Car, 13", by Wolverine, made in USA

Good	Excellent	Mint
$100	**$150**	**$220**

'51 Chevy Bank, 8"

Good	Excellent	Mint
$60	**$100**	**$150**

'57 Ford Convertible, 11 1/2", custom by Lennie, made in USA

Mint
$500

Pressed Steel Automobiles

Cord, 13", by Wyandotte, made in USA

Good	Excellent	Mint
$300	$600	$800

Red Convertible, 10", by Wyandotte, made in USA

Good	Excellent	Mint
$65	$90	$160

Coupe, 18", by Chein-Hercules, made in USA

Good	Excellent	Mint
$500	$800	$1200

Coupe, 18", by Chein-Hercules, made in USA

Good	Excellent	Mint
$500	$800	$1200

Pressed Steel Automobiles

Roadster, 10 1/2", made in USA

Good	Excellent	Mint
$150	$250	-

Coupe, 18", made in USA

Good	Excellent	Mint
$800	$1200	-

Roadster, 19", made in USA

Good	Excellent	Mint
$1000	$1500	-

Coupe, 12 1/4", made in USA

Good	Excellent	Mint
$150	$225	$375

Pressed Steel Automobiles

Coupe, 14", made in USA

Good	Excellent	Mint
$150	**$250**	**$375**

Wyandotte Toy Sedan, 15 1/4",
by All Metal Products Co,
made in USA

Good	Excellent	Mint
$150	**$225**	**$300**

Four Door Sedan, 10",
mechanical action, made in
USA

Good	Excellent	Mint
$75	**$120**	**$175**

Die Cast Automobiles

'57 Cadillac, 8", by Banthrico
Inc., made in USA

Good	Excellent	Mint
$45	**$100**	**$150**

'51 Buick Super Bank, 8",
by Banthrico Inc., made in
USA

Good	Excellent	Mint
$45	**$100**	**$140**

'49 Ford Bank, 7 3/4", by
Banthrico Inc., made in
USA

Good	Excellent	Mint
$45	**$90**	**$120**

'50 Chevy Bank, 7 3/4", by
Banthrico Inc., made in USA

Good	Excellent	Mint
$65	**$120**	**$175**

Die Cast Automobiles

Coupe, 12 1/2", by Playmate
Toys, made in USA

Good	Excellent	Mint
$85	**$100**	**$165**

Convertible, 12 1/2", by
Playmate Toys, made in
USA

Good	Excellent	Mint
$85	**$100**	**$165**

Jaguar, 17 1/2", by Doepke,
made in USA

Good	Excellent	Mint
$200	**$350**	**$485**

M.G., 15 1/2", by Doepke,
made in USA

Good	Excellent	Mint
$200	**$300**	**$400**

Die Cast Automobiles

Hot Rod, 9", by All American Co., made in USA

Good	Excellent	Mint
$200	**$350**	**$450**

Roadster, 10 1/4", by Faith Mfg., made in USA

Good	Excellent	Mint
$100	**$165**	**$230**

'69 Dodge Daytona, 5 1/4", by Mae, made in Canada

Mint
$100

Tin Automobiles

Coupe, 10 1/2", made in
Germany

Good	Excellent	Mint
$200	**$400**	**$600**

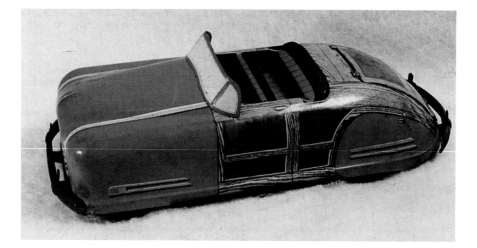

Woody Convertible, 12 3/4",
by Wyandotte, made in
USA

Good	Excellent	Mint
$100	**$150**	**$200**

Four Door Sedan, 9 3/8",
wind-up, made in Germany

Good	Excellent	Mint
$900	**$1500**	**$1900**

Wind-Up Automobiles

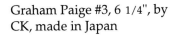

Bumper Car, 4 1/2", by JRD, made in France

Good	Excellent	Mint
$80	$110	$160

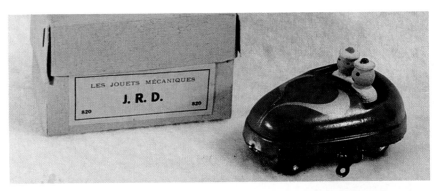

Graham Paige #3, 6 1/4", by CK, made in Japan

Good	Excellent	Mint
$200	$300	$500

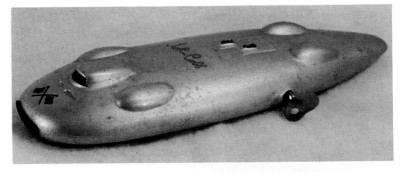

Land Speed Record Race Car, 10 1/2"

Good	Excellent	Mint
$100	$175	$250

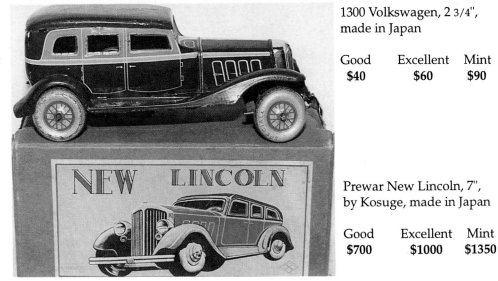

1300 Volkswagen, 2 3/4", made in Japan

Good	Excellent	Mint
$40	$60	$90

Prewar New Lincoln, 7", by Kosuge, made in Japan

Good	Excellent	Mint
$700	$1000	$1350

Miscellaneous Battery Operated Vehicles

Corvette Race Car #33, 10 1/4", by Taiyo, made in Japan

Good	Excellent	Mint
$85	$110	$145

Cadillac Stunt Car, 11 1/4", by Modern Toys, made in Japan

Good	Excellent	Mint
$45	$80	$120

Ford Pantera, 10", made in Japan

Good	Excellent	Mint
$85	$130	$165

Two Man Dream Car, 11 1/2", made in Japan

Good	Excellent	Mint
$150	$260	$350

Miscellaneous Battery Operated Vehicles

Mongoose Hot Rod, 10 1/4",
by Taiyo, made in Japan

Good	Excellent	Mint
$100	$125	$160

Mustang Mach 1, 10 1/2", by
Taiyo, made in Japan

Good	Excellent	Mint
$75	$100	$150

Mustang, 9 1/2", by Taiyo,
made in Japan

Good	Excellent	Mint
$75	$100	$140

Miscellaneous Battery Operated Vehicles

Corvette Stingray, 10 1/4", by Taiyo, made in Japan

Good	Excellent	Mint
$75	**$100**	**$145**

Corvette Stingray, 10 1/4", by Taiyo, made in Japan

Good	Excellent	Mint
$75	**$100**	**$145**

Hot Rod, 6", by Bandai, made in Japan

Good	Excellent	Mint
$75	**$125**	**$175**

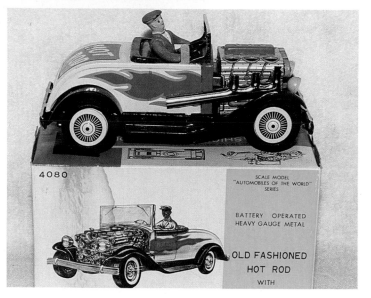

Miscellaneous Battery Operated Vehicles

Excalibur, 10 1/2", by
Daishin, made in Japan

Good	Excellent	Mint
$60	$100	$175

Porsche Carrera 10, 12 1/2",
by ATC, made in Japan

Good	Excellent	Mint
$165	$220	$275

Porsche Race Car 911-S #17,
10", made in Japan

Good	Excellent	Mint
$100	$150	$200

Mustang Stunt Car, 10 1/2", by TPS,
made in Japan

Good	Excellent	Mint
$75	$90	$125

Drag Hot Rod, 8 1/2", made in
Japan

Good	Excellent	Mint
$100	$200	$250

Miscellaneous Battery Operated Vehicles

Porsche Rally Car, 10", by TPS, made in Japan

Good	Excellent	Mint
$100	$150	$200

Chaparral, 11", by Alps, made in Japan

Good	Excellent	Mint
$100	$150	$200

'64 Ford Stock Car #5, 12 1/2", made in Japan

Good	Excellent	Mint
$90	$150	$200

Z-28 Camaro, 10 1/4", by Taiyo, made in Japan

Good	Excellent	Mint
$80	$100	$125

Miscellaneous Japanese Friction Vehicles

'58 Edsel, 9", made in Japan

Good   Excellent   Mint
$300 $500 $750

'58 Mercury, 4 1/2", made in Japan

Good   Excellent   Mint
$30 $45 $65

Roadster, 9", made in Japan

Good   Excellent   Mint
$120 $175 $250

Opel, 7 1/4", made in Japan

Good   Excellent   Mint
$75 $110 $150

Miscellaneous Japanese Friction Vehicles

Isetta, 6 1/4", made in Japan

Good	Excellent	Mint
$90	$150	$200

'59 Chevy, 11 3/4", by SY, made in Japan

Good	Excellent	Mint
$1000	$1300	$1600

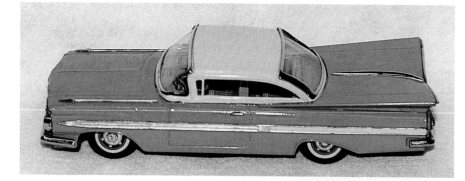

Hot Rod with Duck Driver, 8", by S, made in Japan

Good	Excellent	Mint
$90	$175	$250

Miscellaneous Japanese Friction Vehicles

'62 Chevy, 11", made in Japan

Good	Excellent	Mint
$200	$275	$350

M.G., 8 1/2", by KO, made in Japan

Good	Excellent	Mint
$115	$175	$235

'60 Chevy, 11 3/4", by Marusan, made in Japan

Good	Excellent	Mint
$900	$1200	$1500

Shooting Star, 8", by TT, made in Japan

Good	Excellent	Mint
$225	$300	$450

29

Miscellaneous Japanese Friction Vehicles

'60 Chevy Convertible, 11 1/2",
made in Japan

Good	Excellent	Mint
$600	**$1100**	**$1550**

Buick Convertible, 8 3/4",
made in Japan

Good	Excellent	Mint
$100	**$165**	**$210**

M.G. Convertible, 10 1/2",
made in Japan

Good	Excellent	Mint
$800	**$1100**	**$1400**

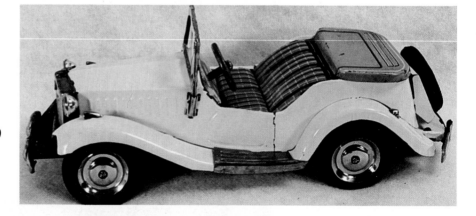

Doll in Car, 7 3/8", made in
Japan

Good	Excellent	Mint
$35	**$70**	**$100**

Miscellaneous Japanese Friction Vehicles

'53 Dodge, 9", by TM, made in Japan

Good	Excellent	Mint
$50	$125	$165

Cadillac, 8", made in Japan

Good	Excellent	Mint
$80	$100	$125

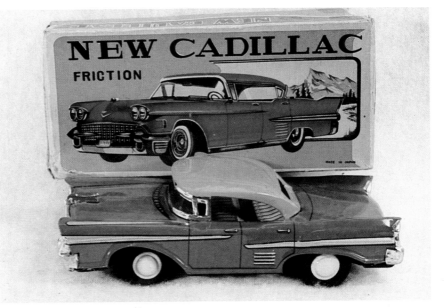

M.G. Convertible, 6 1/2", made in Japan

Good	Excellent	Mint
$80	$110	$150

Miscellaneous Japanese Friction Vehicles

Volkswagen Beetle, 7 1/4",
made in Japan

Good	Excellent	Mint
$80	**$120**	**$150**

'55 Buick, 7 1/2", made in
Japan

Good	Excellent	Mint
$70	**$100**	**$160**

'56 Lincoln with Dog, 7 1/2",
made in Japan

Good	Excellent	Mint
$75	**$125**	**$200**

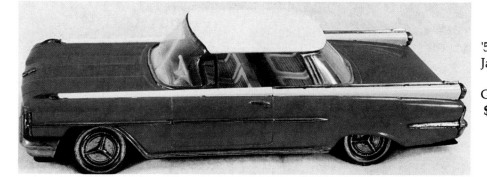

'59 Oldsmobile, 13", made in
Japan

Good	Excellent	Mint
$300	**$450**	**$585**

Miscellaneous Japanese Friction Vehicles

Volvo, 8", made in Japan

Good	Excellent	Mint
$120	**$175**	**$250**

Jaguar 140, 7 1/2", made in Japan

Good	Excellent	Mint
$100	**$140**	**$175**

Capri, 11", by Aoshin, made in Japan

Good	Excellent	Mint
$65	**$110**	**$170**

Citroen, 5 1/4", made in Japan

Good	Excellent	Mint
$65	**$90**	**$135**

'55 Pontiac, 7", made in Japan

Good	Excellent	Mint
$75	**$100**	**$135**

Miscellaneous Japanese Friction Vehicles

Volkswagen Beetle, 8 1/4",
by Arnold, made in Japan

Good	Excellent	Mint
$150	**$250**	**$325**

'58 Lincoln, 9", made in Japan

Good	Excellent	Mint
$60	**$100**	**$140**

'58 Edsel, 8 3/4", made in Japan

Good	Excellent	Mint
$200	**$375**	**$500**

'55 Studebaker, 9", made in Japan

Good	Excellent	Mint
$90	**$160**	**$225**

Miscellaneous Japanese Friction Vehicles

Volvo, 7 1/2", made in Japan

Good	Excellent	Mint
$150	**$250**	**$325**

'59 Ford Convertible with Retractable Top, 11", made in Japan

Good	Excellent	Mint
$120	**$275**	**$400**

'58 Lincoln, 9", made in Japan

Good	Excellent	Mint
$60	**$100**	**$140**

'51 Cadillac, 11 1/2", by Alps, made in Japan

Good	Excellent	Mint
$600	**$1100**	**$1500**

Miscellaneous Japanese Friction Vehicles

'58 Oldsmobile, 12", by Yonezawa, made in Japan

Good	Excellent	Mint
$500	$900	$1200

Citroen, 5", by Yonezawa, made in Japan

Good	Excellent	Mint
$50	$75	$100

'60 Ford Convertibles, 11", by Haji, made in Japan

Good	Excellent	Mint
$200	$350	$500

'59 Chevy, 8 1/2", by ATC, made in Japan

Good	Excellent	Mint
$100	$150	$225

Miscellaneous Japanese Friction Vehicles

Break Apart Stunt Car, 8 1/4",
by ATC, made in Japan

Good	Excellent	Mint
$90	$140	$175

'67 Camaro with Bucket
Seats, 13 1/2", by TK, made
in Japan

Good	Excellent	Mint
$275	$400	$500

Speedking #10, 6 1/2", by
Cragstan

Good	Excellent	Mint
$40	$60	$80

Mercury, 8", by K, made in
Japan

Good	Excellent	Mint
$120	$180	$250

Bandai Friction Vehicles

Lotus, 8 1/2", made in Japan

Good	Excellent	Mint
$90	$145	$185

'63 Thunderbird, 8 1/4", made in Japan

Good	Excellent	Mint
$100	$140	$180

Triumph TR-3, 8 1/4", made in Japan

Good	Excellent	Mint
$90	$120	$175

Cadillac, 11 1/4", made in Japan

Good	Excellent	Mint
$90	$200	$300

Bandai Friction Vehicles

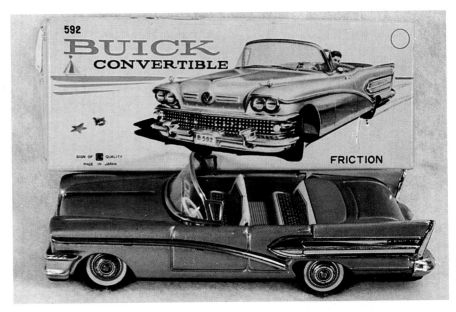

'58 Buick, 8 1/4", made in Japan

Good	Excellent	Mint
$150	$200	$250

Cadillac, 11 1/2", made in Japan

Good	Excellent	Mint
$90	$200	$300

Cadillac Convertible with Bucket Seats, 17", made in Japan

Good	Excellent	Mint
$450	$725	$950

Cadillac Convertible, 17", made in Japan

Good	Excellent	Mint
$450	$725	$950

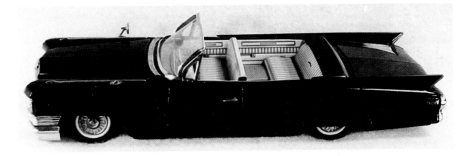

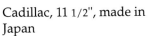

Bandai Friction Vehicles

Cadillac, 11 1/4", made in Japan

Good	Excellent	Mint
$90	$200	$300

'58 Chevy Impala, 6 1/4", made in Japan

Good	Excellent	Mint
$95	$135	$175

Mustang, 13", made in Japan

Good	Excellent	Mint
$80	$100	$140

Rolls Royce Silver Cloud, 11 3/4", made in Japan

Good	Excellent	Mint
$180	$325	$500

Bandai Friction Vehicles

'58 Ford Convertible, 8",
made in Japan

Good   Excellent   Mint
$85   **$120**   **$160**

'59 Cadillac, 11 1/2", made
in Japan

Good   Excellent   Mint
$100   **$200**   **$300**

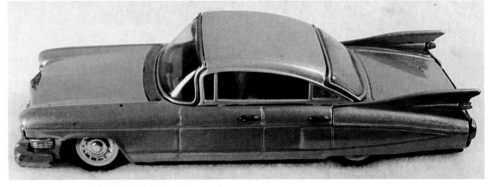

Mustang, 7 1/8", made in
Japan

Good   Excellent   Mint
$70   **$100**   **$160**

'59 Cadillac, 11 1/4", made in
Japan

Good   Excellent   Mint
$150   **$250**   **$350**

Bandai Friction Vehicles

'64 Cadillac, 17", made in Japan

Good	Excellent	Mint
$400	**$625**	**$775**

Hot Rod, 8 3/4", made in Japan

Good	Excellent	Mint
$80	**$110**	**$175**

'58 Chevy Impala, 6 1/4", made in Japan

Good	Excellent	Mint
$95	**$135**	**$175**

Bandai Friction Vehicles

'61 Chevy, 11", made in Japan

Good	Excellent	Mint
$225	**$300**	**$450**

'59 Cadillac, 11 1/2", made in Japan

Good	Excellent	Mint
$100	**$200**	**$300**

'65 Mustang, 11 1/4", made in Japan

Good	Excellent	Mint
$120	**$185**	**$225**

'59 Cadillac, 11 1/2", made in Japan

Good	Excellent	Mint
$125	**$225**	**$325**

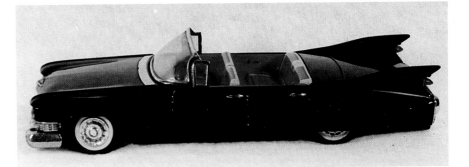

Bandai Friction Vehicles

'58 Chevy Convertible, 8 1/2",
made in Japan

Good	Excellent	Mint
$100	**$135**	**$165**

Corvette Stingray, 8 1/4",
made in Japan

Good	Excellent	Mint
$90	**$125**	**$175**

MGA 1600, 8 1/4", made in
Japan

Good	Excellent	Mint
$100	**$175**	**$225**

Mercedes 230, 8 1/4", made
in Japan

Good	Excellent	Mint
$85	**$110**	**$160**

Bandai Friction Vehicles

Imperial Convertible, 8 1/2",
made in Japan

Good	Excellent	Mint
$80	**$140**	**$170**

Lincoln Continental, 11 3/4",
made in Japan

Good	Excellent	Mint
$100	**$190**	**$285**

'60 Cadillac, 11 1/2", made in
Japan

Good	Excellent	Mint
$90	**$200**	**$300**

Bandai Friction Vehicles

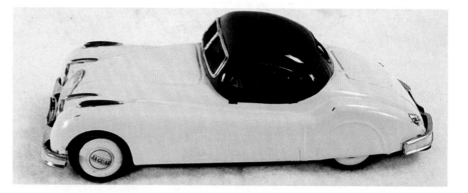

Jaguar, 9 1/2", made in Japan

Good | Excellent | Mint
$200 | $300 | $400

'65 Mustang, 8 1/4", made in Japan

Good | Excellent | Mint
$65 | $100 | $130

Cougar, 10", made in Japan

Good | Excellent | Mint
$80 | $100 | $140

'56 Chevy Convertible, 9 3/4", made in Japan

Good | Excellent | Mint
$120 | $225 | $300

Bandai Friction Vehicles

Corvette, 7", made in Japan

Good	Excellent	Mint
$125	**$200**	**$300**

'56 Ford Fairlane Sunliner, 12", made in Japan

Good	Excellent	Mint
$350	**$500**	**$600**

'59 Cadillac (rare two tone), 11 1/2", made in Japan

Good	Excellent	Mint
$200	**$300**	**$375**

Bandai Friction Vehicles

'54 MG, 10 1/2", made in Japan

Good	Excellent	Mint
$800	**$1100**	**$1400**

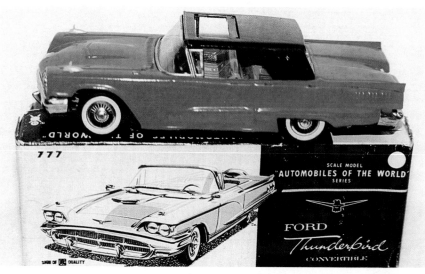

'60 Thunderbird with sliding roof, 8", made in Japan

Good	Excellent	Mint
$85	**$120**	**$145**

'64 Chevelle, 8 1/4", made in Japan

Good	Excellent	Mint
$75	**$110**	**$165**

Renault Dauphine, 8", made in Japan

Good	Excellent	Mint
$120	**$150**	**$185**

Bandai Friction Vehicles

Rolls Royce, 11 3/4", made in Japan

Good	Excellent	Mint
$160	$350	$575

'56 Chevy El Camino, 9 3/4", made in Japan

Good	Excellent	Mint
$80	$125	$175

MG Racer, 8 1/4", made in Japan

Good	Excellent	Mint
$80	$175	$225

Hot Rod #7, 8", made in Japan

Good	Excellent	Mint
$70	$125	$185

TN Friction Vehicles

'58 Ford (retractable), 7 1/2",
made in Japan

Good	Excellent	Mint
$70	$140	$190

Honda 600, 9 3/4", made in
Japan

Good	Excellent	Mint
$85	$125	$185

Hot Rod Century, 7 1/4",
made in Japan

Good	Excellent	Mint
$70	$125	$185

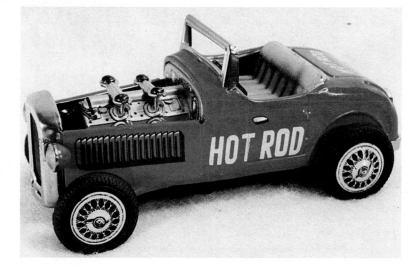

TN Friction Vehicles

Hot Rod, 7 3/4", made in Japan

Good	Excellent	Mint
$150	**$180**	**$225**

'65 Cadillac, 25 1/2", made in Japan

Good	Excellent	Mint
$350	**$700**	**$900**

'61 Buick, 16", made in Japan

Good	Excellent	Mint
$350	**$500**	**$650**

Custom '65 Mustang Shelby GT, 15 3/4", by Lennie and TN, made in Japan

Good	Excellent	Mint
-	-	**$350**

TN Friction Vehicles

Mercedes Benz, 8 1/2",
made in Japan

Good	Excellent	Mint
$80	$120	$165

'59 Buick, 11 1/2", made in
Japan

Good	Excellent	Mint
$165	$250	$335

'58 Ford (retractable), 7 1/2",
made in Japan

Good	Excellent	Mint
$80	$100	$150

Y and Ichiko Friction Vehicles

Mercedes Benz 250 SE, 13 1/2",
by Ichiko, made in Japan

Good	Excellent	Mint
$200	$250	$325

'61 Thunderbird Stock Car #27,
9", by Ichiko, made in Japan

Good	Excellent	Mint
$90	$150	$180

Valiant with opening hood, 9
1/4", by Y, made in Japan

Good	Excellent	Mint
$90	$140	$175

Zephyr Fat Car, 11", by Y,
made in Japan

Good	Excellent	Mint
$110	$200	$250

Y and Ichiko Friction Vehicles

'55 Cadillac, 7 1/2", by Y, made in Japan

Good   Excellent   Mint
$40   **$70**   **$100**

Crown Fat Car, 11", by Y, made in Japan

Good   Excellent   Mint
$50   **$100**   **$150**

Renault Dauphine, 8", by Y, made in Japan

Good   Excellent   Mint
$90   **$130**   **$160**

Y and Ichiko Friction Vehicles

Lincoln Sun Deck Convertibles, 7 1/2", by Y, made in Japan

Good	Excellent	Mint
$210	**$330**	**$425**

'57 Ford, 8", by Ichiko, made in Japan

Good	Excellent	Mint
$70	**$120**	**$180**

Mercedes 230 SL Coupe with opening doors, 9 1/4", by Ichiko, made in Japan

Good	Excellent	Mint
$100	**$175**	**$225**

Datsun Fairlady Z Coupe, 17 1/2", by Ichiko, made in Japan

Good	Excellent	Mint
$160	**$200**	**$275**

Japanese Battery Operated Vehicles

'67 Camaro, 10", by Taiyo, made in Japan

Good	Excellent	Mint
$80	$130	$160

Toronado, 11", made in Japan

Good	Excellent	Mint
$90	$125	$165

'65 Cadillac, 10 3/4", by Bandai, made in Japan

Good	Excellent	Mint
$60	$100	$200

'65 Mustang, 11 3/4", by Bandai, made in Japan

Good	Excellent	Mint
$80	$135	$175

Toronado, 10 1/4", made in Japan

Good	Excellent	Mint
$65	$100	$135

Japanese Battery Operated Vehicles

Mercedes Benz, 11", made in Japan

Good	Excellent	Mint
$100	**$220**	**$300**

Porsche, 10 3/4", by TT, made in Japan

Good	Excellent	Mint
$150	**$275**	**$375**

Toronado, 10 1/4", made in Japan

Good	Excellent	Mint
$80	**$100**	**$140**

Corvette, 10 1/2", made in Japan

Good	Excellent	Mint
$90	**$140**	**$165**

Volkswagen Convertible, 9 3/4", made in Japan

Good	Excellent	Mint
$275	**$425**	**$585**

Japanese Battery Operated Vehicles

Smokey Bill and Old Car, 9 1/4",
by Modern Toys, made in Japan

Good	Excellent	Mint
$45	**$75**	**$125**

Lincoln Mark II, 9 1/2", by
KS, made in Japan

Good	Excellent	Mint
$90	**$150**	**$225**

Cadillac Open Car, 6 1/2",
made in Japan

Good	Excellent	Mint
$40	**$80**	**$100**

Japanese Battery Operated Vehicles

Volkswagen Beetle Convertible, 10", made in Japan

Good	Excellent	Mint
$275	**$425**	**$585**

Old Car with Driver, 9",
made in Japan

Good	Excellent	Mint
$60	**$90**	**$125**

Old Fashioned Car, 9 1/4", by
TN, made in Japan

Good	Excellent	Mint
$25	**$50**	**$75**

Japanese Battery Operated Vehicles

'66 Dodge Charger, 16", by TN, made in Japan

Good	Excellent	Mint
$150	**$240**	**$300**

Waddles Bear Family Car, 6 1/2", by Y, made in Japan

Good	Excellent	Mint
$20	**$50**	**$85**

Chrysler, 7", by TN, made in Japan

Good	Excellent	Mint
$100	**$150**	**$200**

Japanese Battery Operated Vehicles

'65 Mustang Retractable Convertible, 13 1/2", by Y, made in Japan

Good	Excellent	Mint
$110	**$230**	**$350**

Hot Rod, 10 1/4", by Alps, made in Japan

Good	Excellent	Mint
$65	**$125**	**$175**

Mustang with Passengers, 13 1/2", by Alps, made in Japan

Good	Excellent	Mint
$170	**$300**	**$385**

Japanese Battery Operated Vehicles

Corvair Bertone, 12 1/4", by Bandai, made in Japan

Good	Excellent	Mint
$200	$350	$500

'53 Plymouth Convertible, 9 1/2", made in Japan

Good	Excellent	Mint
$125	$250	$350

Porsche with Opening Doors, 10 1/2", by Bandai, made in Japan

Good	Excellent	Mint
$85	$150	$250

Ferrari, 11 1/4", by Bandai, made in Japan

Good	Excellent	Mint
$200	$350	$425

Japanese Battery Operated Vehicles

Mercedes Benz 220, 10 1/2",
by Bandai, made in Japan

Good	Excellent	Mint
$165	$220	$275

Excalibur, 10", by Bandai,
made in Japan

Good	Excellent	Mint
$60	$80	$140

Volkswagen Beetle, 10 1/2",
by Bandai, made in Japan

Good	Excellent	Mint
$65	$100	$125

Miscellaneous Japanese Vehicles

Cadillac, 12 1/2", by
Marusan, made in Japan

Good   Excellent   Mint
$450   **$700**   **$900**

Mercedes Benz with
Transparent Hood, 8 1/2",
made in Japan

Good   Excellent   Mint
$75   **$135**   **$185**

'56 Buick, 8 1/2", made in
Japan

Good   Excellent   Mint
$100   **$150**   **$185**

Miscellaneous Japanese Vehicles

Corvettes, 6 1/2", by Tonka, made in Japan

Good	Excellent	Mint
$20	$40	$60

Various Vehicles, 4 1/2", made in Japan

Complete Set:
$150

'63 Ford Stock Car #27, 13 3/4", by K, made in Japan

Good	Excellent	Mint
$40	$70	$90

Pontiac Fat Car, 14 1/2", made in Japan

Good	Excellent	Mint
$300	$500	$800

Vehicles With Trailers

'59 Ford with Boat and
Trailer, 16 1/2", by Haji,
made in Japan

Good	Excellent	Mint
$150	**$200**	**$275**

'60 Chevy with Racer and
Trailer, 9 7/8", by Tootsietoy,
made in USA

Good	Excellent	Mint
$15	**$30**	**$45**

Ford Pickup with Camper
and Trailer, 5 5/8", by Midge
Toy, made in USA

Good	Excellent	Mint
$10	**$30**	**$40**

Car with Camper Trailer, 18
5/8", wind-up, made in
England

Good	Excellent	Mint
$175	**$275**	**$425**

Car with Trailer, 23 1/2",
pressed steel, by Kingsbury,
made in USA

Good	Excellent	Mint
$200	**$300**	**$600**

Vehicles With Trailers

'57 Ford with Boat and Trailer, 16", friction powered, by Haji, made in Japan

Good	Excellent	Mint
$150	**$240**	**$300**

Station Wagon with Boat and Trailer, 11 1/2", friction powered, made in Japan

Good	Excellent	Mint
$75	**$100**	**$150**

'59 Mercury Convertible with U-Haul Trailer, 15", friction powered, made in Japan

Good	Excellent	Mint
$60	**$100**	**$125**

Car and Camper, 16", wind-up, by Mettoy, made in Great Britain

Good	Excellent	Mint
$150	**$250**	**$350**

'59 Ford with Trailer and Boat, 21 1/4", by Y, made in Japan

Good	Excellent	Mint
$75	**$185**	**$350**

Vehicles With Trailers

'64 Chevelle with House Trailer, 17 1/4", battery operated, by Bandai, made in Japan

Good	Excellent	Mint
$110	**$185**	**$240**

Speedway Special, 16 1/2", friction powered, by Linemar, made in Japan

Good	Excellent	Mint
$170	**$250**	**$340**

Camper Truck with Boat and Trailer, 15", by Buddy L, made in USA

Good	Excellent	Mint
$90	**$150**	**$240**

Vehicles With Trailers

Mercedes Benz with Camper, 22 1/2", plastic, friction powered, by GAMA, made in Germany

Good	Excellent	Mint
$90	$175	$250

Seven Piece Vacation Set, by Cragstan, made in Japan

Good	Excellent	Mint
$300	$450	$600

Car and Camper, 11 1/2", pressed steel, by Wyandotte, made in USA

Good	Excellent	Mint
$90	$150	$200

Car and Camper, 11", pressed steel, by Wyandotte, made in USA

Good	Excellent	Mint
$95	$150	$200

Station Wagon with Teepee Camper, 24 1/2", by Buddy L, made in USA

Good	Excellent	Mint
$100	$150	$200

Station Wagons

'60 Ford "Standard Coffee" Galazie, 11 1/2", friction powered, made in Japan

Good	Excellent	Mint
$1100	$1850	$2450

'69 Chevy, 7", friction powered, by Bandi Line, made in Korea

Good	Excellent	Mint
$80	$110	$165

'56 Pontiac, 8", friction powered, made in Japan

Good	Excellent	Mint
$100	$140	$170

'60 Chevy Bel Air, 10", friction powered, by ATC, made in Japan

Good	Excellent	Mint
$85	$140	$175

'57 Ford, 7 3/4", friction powered, made in Japan

Good	Excellent	Mint
$75	$100	$150

Station Wagons

'62 Ford Falcon Squire, 8 3/4",
friction powered, by Alps,
made in Japan

Good   Excellent   Mint
$70 $120 $165

Checker Marathon Station
Wagon, 7", battery oper-
ated, made in Japan

Good   Excellent   Mint
$75 $100 $135

'60 Chevy Bel Air, 10", friction
powered, by ATC, made in
Japan

Good   Excellent   Mint
$125 $200 $300

'58 Oldsmobile Super 88, 7",
made in Japan

Good   Excellent   Mint
$85 $120 $150

Station Wagons

'52 Rambler, 9 1/2", friction powered, by Marusan, made in Japan

Good	Excellent	Mint
$125	**$200**	**$300**

Toytown Estate Station Wagon, 21 1/6", by Wyandotte, made in USA

Good	Excellent	Mint
$200	**$400**	**$600**

'52 Rambler, 10", friction powered, made in Japan

Good	Excellent	Mint
$125	**$160**	**$200**

Station Wagons

Plymouth, 8 1/4", friction powered, by Bandai, made in Japan

Good	Excellent	Mint
$110	**$150**	**$185**

Ford, 12", friction powered, by Bandai, made in Japan

Good	Excellent	Mint
$90	**$180**	**$250**

Opel Rekord, 8 1/4", friction powered, by Bandai, made in Japan

Good	Excellent	Mint
$85	**$130**	**$165**

'57 Mercury, 8", friction powered, by Bandai, made in Japan

Good	Excellent	Mint
$70	**$120**	**$150**

'57 Ford Fairlane 500 with Small Boat, 6 1/2", friction powered, made in Japan

Good	Excellent	Mint
$90	**$150**	**$225**

Station Wagons

'63 Ford, 15", by Buddy L, made in USA

Good	Excellent	Mint
$65	$100	$150

'62 Rambler with Luggage Rack and Ski Equipment, 11", by Bandai, made in Japan

Good	Excellent	Mint
$120	$220	$300

'58 Chevy, 6 1/4", friction powered, by Bandai, made in Japan

Good	Excellent	Mint
$85	$130	$175

Taxicabs

Taxi Cabs, 7", by
Hubley, made in USA

Mint Set with Box
$400

Taxi, 12 1/2", friction
powered, by Wolverine,
made in USA

Good   Excellent   Mint
$75   **$125**   **$175**

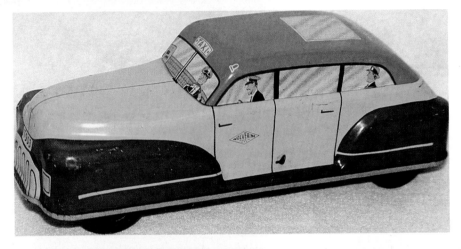

'67 Dodge Dart Checker Cab,
12", friction powered, by TN,
made in Japan

Good   Excellent   Mint
$150   **$220**   **$300**

Peugot 404 Taxi, 11 3/4",
battery operated, by Joustra,
made in France

Good   Excellent   Mint
$300   **$450**   **$600**

Taxicabs

'64 Plymouth Pan-Am Airport Service Car, 10", friction powered, by Y, made in Japan

Good	Excellent	Mint
$90	$140	$190

Bluebird Taxi, 8", cast iron, by Arcade, made in USA

Good	Excellent	Mint
$1800	$3000	$5000

Yellow Cab Express, 26", pressed steel, by Cowdery, made in USA

Mint
$1500

Taxicabs

Airport Limousine, 8 5/8",
friction powered, made in
Japan

Good	Excellent	Mint
$40	**$75**	**$100**

'55 Buick Taxi, 7 1/2", remote
control, by Linemar Toys,
made in Japan

Good	Excellent	Mint
$85	**$120**	**$150**

Lincoln Airport Limousine,
9", friction powered, by
Cragstan, made in Japan

Good	Excellent	Mint
$75	**$125**	**$160**

Ford Taunus Körskola, 9 1/4",
battery operated, by Ichiko,
made in Japan

Good	Excellent	Mint
$80	**$125**	**$170**

Marx Vehicles

G-Man Car, 12 3/4", wind-
up, battery operated, made
in USA

Good	Excellent	Mint
$125	**$170**	**$225**

Greyhound, 6", pressed
steel, made in USA

Good	Excellent	Mint
$100	**$175**	**$275**

Dottie the Driver, 6 3/4",
wind-up, made in USA

Good	Excellent	Mint
$85	**$120**	**$170**

Marx Vehicles

Careful Johnnie, 6 3/4",
wind-up, made in USA

Good	Excellent	Mint
$85	**$120**	**$170**

Hot Rod Coupe, 7 1/4", friction
powered, made in Japan

Good	Excellent	Mint
$90	**$120**	**$165**

Nutty Mad Car, 9 1/4",
battery operated, made in
Japan

Good	Excellent	Mint
$100	**$300**	**$450**

Wind-Up Racers

Racer #1, 9 1/2", by Schuco, made in Germany

Good	Excellent	Mint
$100	**$150**	**$200**

Race Car #5, 10 3/4", by Dubigo Mfg., made in USA

Good	Excellent	Mint
$75	**$125**	**$160**

Racers #3 & #4, 8 1/4", plastic, by Saunders, made in USA

Good	Excellent	Mint
$30	**$60**	**$80**

Racer #1, 10", plastic, by Glen Dimension Co., made in USA

Good	Excellent	Mint
$50	**$90**	**$135**

Wind-Up Racers

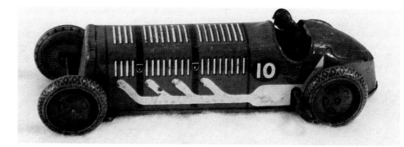

Racer #10, 8 3/4", made in England

Good	Excellent	Mint
$125	**$200**	**$265**

Racer #3, 8 1/4", made in France

Good	Excellent	Mint
$100	**$150**	**$200**

Racer #8, 6"

Good	Excellent	Mint
$150	**$200**	**$275**

Mormac "Firefly" Racer, 10", by Normac Mfg., made in USA

Good	Excellent	Mint
$75	**$110**	**$150**

Wind-Up Racers

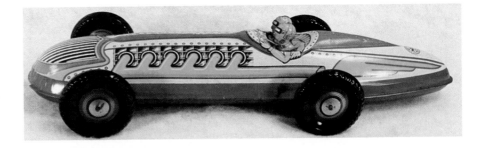

Two Man Racer, 16 1/2", by Marx, made in USA

Good	Excellent	Mint
$200	$300	$425

Racer #1, 13", by Marx, made in USA

Good	Excellent	Mint
$100	$185	$250

Speed King Racer, 16 1/2", by Marx, made in USA

Good	Excellent	Mint
$225	$325	$450

Racer #12, 16", by Marx, made in USA

Good	Excellent	Mint
$200	$275	$350

Red Flash Racer #31, 9 1/2", by Strauss, made in USA

Good	Excellent	Mint
$375	$500	$650

Miscellaneous Racers

Racer #2, 10 3/4", diecast, by R. Roach Industries, made in USA

Good	Excellent	Mint
$45	$80	$120

Racer #34, 11 3/4"

Good	Excellent	Mint
$110	$170	$225

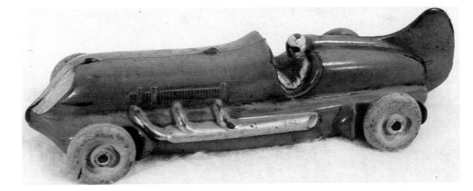

Racer, 11", rubber, by Auburn Rubber Co., made in USA

Good	Excellent	Mint
$30	$60	$120

Racer, 16 1/2", diecast, made in USA

Good	Excellent	Mint
$45	$80	$120

Thimbledrome Champion Racers, 9 1/2", by Ray Cox, made in USA

Good	Excellent	Mint
$150	$250	$300

Miscellaneous Racers

Racer #20, 10 1/4", by Elenee Toys Inc., made in USA

Good	Excellent	Mint
$80	$100	$150

See-Thru Micro Racer #1005, 5 1/2", by Schuco, made in Germany

Good	Excellent	Mint
$100	$200	$300

Race Car #16, 11 1/4", made in France

Good	Excellent	Mint
$80	$110	$145

Racer #7, 12 3/4", made in England

Good	Excellent	Mint
$300	$400	$500

Racer #46, 16 1/2", by Sturm, made in USA

$1500

Miscellaneous Racers

Racer #17, 18 1/2", by Sturm, made in USA

$1500

Scientific Gas Powered Model, 9", made in USA

Good	Excellent	Mint
$50	**$80**	**$100**

Racer O'Boy, 19", by Kiddies Metal, made in USA

Good	Excellent	Mint
$800	**$1200**	**$1700**

Miscellaneous Racers

Racer, 18", gas powered, by
Hiller, made in USA

Good   Excellent   Mint
$650   **$1000**   **$1500**

Bugatti Racer,
15", by JK 1991

Mint
$4500

Racer #6, 12 1/2", by Marx,
made in USA

Good   Excellent   Mint
$150   **$200**   **$350**

Racer #8, 12 1/2", by Marx,
made in USA

Good   Excellent   Mint
$150   **$200**   **$350**

Miscellaneous Racers

Racer #3, 7 1/4", made in France

Good	Excellent	Mint
$165	**$225**	**$300**

Racer #35, 20", by Marx, made in USA

Good	Excellent	Mint
$85	**$150**	**$250**

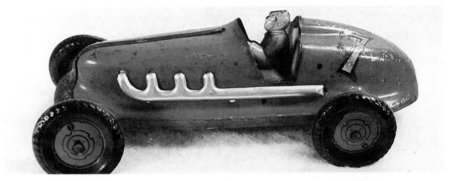

Racer #7, 12 1/2", by Marx, made in USA

Good	Excellent	Mint
$150	**$200**	**$350**

Racer #7, 12 1/2", by Marx, made in USA

Good	Excellent	Mint
$150	**$200**	**$350**

Racer #8, 12 1/2", by Marx, made in USA

Good	Excellent	Mint
$150	**$200**	**$350**

Miscellaneous Racers

Diamond Racer, 15 1/2", by
Y, made in Japan

Good   Excellent   Mint
$325   **$550**   **$675**

Mercedes Benz Racer #28, 10 3/4",
by Marklin, made in Germany

Mint
$400

Remote Control Vehicles

Mercedes Benz Gull Wing, 9",
made in Japan

Good	Excellent	Mint
$120	**$200**	**$250**

'58 Ford Retractable
Convertible, 11", made in
Japan

Good	Excellent	Mint
$85	**$200**	**$300**

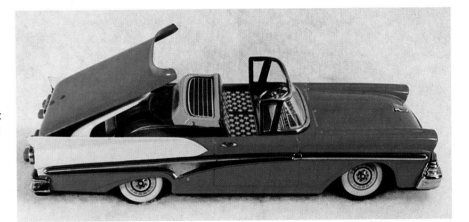

Jaguar, 7 1/2", by Modern
Toys, made in Japan

Good	Excellent	Mint
$80	**$110**	**$165**

Fire Department Vehicles

Fire Engine, 11 1/2", by
Hubley, made in USA

Good	Excellent	Mint
$40	$90	$140

Fire Engine with Hose Reel,
26", pressed steel, by Buddy L,
made in USA

Good	Excellent	Mint
$1150	$1850	-

Water Tower Truck, 21 1/2",
pressed steel, by Keystone,
made in USA

Good	Excellent	Mint
$250	$400	$700

Fire Department Vehicles

Fire Engine, 35", pressed steel, by Doepke Model Toys, made in USA

Good	Excellent	Mint
$110	$200	$300

Fire Engine, 27", by Wyandotte, made in USA

Good	Excellent	Mint
$125	$175	$275

Fire Engine, 31 1/2", by Tonka, made in USA

Good	Excellent	Mint
$150	$200	$240

Fire Engine, 18 1/2", by Hubley, made in USA

Good	Excellent	Mint
$85	$110	$140

Fire Engine, 36 1/2", by Lumar-Marx, made in USA

Good	Excellent	Mint
$125	$200	$300

Fire Department Vehicles

Fire Engine, 10 3/4", battery operated, made in Japan

Good	Excellent	Mint
$90	**$150**	**$200**

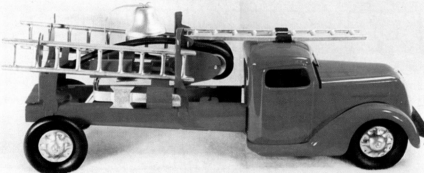

'38 Dodge, 18 1/2", pressed steel, made in USA

Good	Excellent	Mint
$95	**$175**	**$250**

Fire Engine, 13 1/2", battery operated, by Yonezawa, made in Japan

Good	Excellent	Mint
$80	**$110**	**$140**

Fire Department Vehicles

Fire Engine, 8", friction powered, by K, made in Japan

Good	Excellent	Mint
$75	**$125**	**$175**

Fire Engine, 29 1/2", pressed steel, by Buddy L, made in USA

Good	Excellent	Mint
$1000	**$1500**	-

Fire Department Vehicles

Mercury Cougar Fire Chief Car, 10", battery operated, by Taiyo, made in Japan

Good	Excellent	Mint
$75	**$100**	**$140**

'59 Oldsmobile Fire Chief Car, 10 1/4", friction powered, made in Japan

Good	Excellent	Mint
$80	**$125**	**$175**

Fire Engine, 8 1/2", friction powered, by TN, made in Japan

Good	Excellent	Mint
$75	**$115**	**$165**

Fire Department Vehicles

'63 Ford Fire Chief Car, 10 3/4",
friction powered, by Taiyo,
made in Japan

Good	Excellent	Mint
$90	$140	$175

'58 Oldsmobile Fire Chief Car,
8 1/2", friction powered, made
in Japan

Good	Excellent	Mint
$100	$150	$185

'61 Buick Fire Chief Car, 16",
friction powered, made in
Japan

Good	Excellent	Mint
$300	$500	$600

Plymouth Fire Chief Car, 9 1/4",
by CK, made in Japan

Good	Excellent	Mint
$50	$80	$110

Fire Department Vehicles

Fire Dept. #B-212 Set, by Tonka, made in USA

Mint Set
$2000

'63 Ford Fire Chief, 10", friction powered, by Taiyo, made in Japan

Good	Excellent	Mint
$75	**$100**	**$150**

'69 Chevy Fire Chief Car, 11", battery operated, by Alps, made in Japan

Good	Excellent	Mint
$135	**$215**	**$280**

Fire Department Vehicles

Fire Truck, 19", pressed steel, by Structo, made in USA

Good	Excellent	Mint
$150	$250	$350

'59 Oldsmobile Fire Dept. Car, 13", battery operated, made in Japan

Good	Excellent	Mint
$200	$350	$450

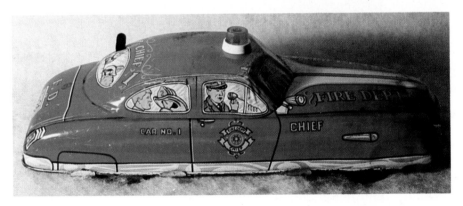

Fire Chief Car #1, 11", by Marx, made in USA

Good	Excellent	Mint
$80	$115	$145

Fire Car #1, 11 1/2", made in Argentina

Good	Excellent	Mint
$75	$90	$125

Fire Department Vehicles

Jeep Fire Engine, 8 1/4", friction powered, made in Japan

Good   Excellent   Mint
$65   **$100**   **$135**

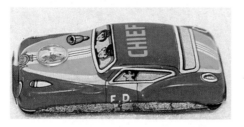

Fire Chief Car with Compass on Hood, 2 3/4", friction powered, made in Japan

Good   Excellent   Mint
$20   **$35**   **$50**

Climbing Fireman, 22 1/4", wind-up, by Marx, made in USA

Good   Excellent   Mint
$90   **$150**   **$200**

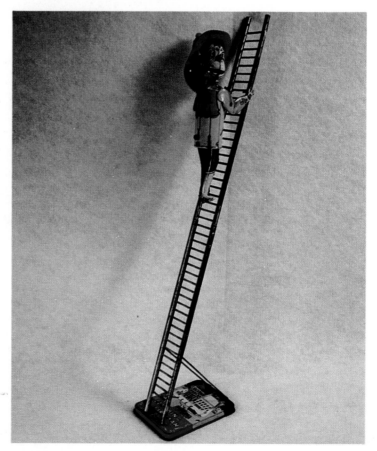

Police Department Vehicles

Porsche Patrol Car, 11", battery operated, by Aoshin, made in Japan

Good	Excellent	Mint
$150	**$250**	**$350**

Siren Patrol Motorcycle, 12", battery operated, by Modern Toys, made in Japan

Good	Excellent	Mint
$100	**$150**	**$225**

Buick Patrol Car, 15 3/8", friction powered, made in Japan

Good	Excellent	Mint
$125	**$225**	**$350**

Police Department Vehicles

Toronado Police Car, 15 1/2",
friction powered, by ATC,
made in Japan

Good	Excellent	Mint
$195	**$320**	**$400**

'58 Oldsmobile Highway
Patrol Car, 8 1/2", friction
powered, made in Japan

Good	Excellent	Mint
$100	**$150**	**$175**

Police Jeep, 13 3/4", battery
operated, by TN, made in
Japan

Good	Excellent	Mint
$100	**$220**	**$285**

Police Department Vehicles

'52 Ford Police Patrol Car, 10 1/4", battery operated, made in Japan

Good	Excellent	Mint
$170	**$275**	**$350**

Highway Patrol Car, 10 1/2", friction powered, made in Japan

Good	Excellent	Mint
$95	**$140**	**$175**

Prewar Police Car and Prewar Small Car, 11" and 4 3/4", made in Japan

Good	Excellent	Mint
$1500	**$3000**	**$4500**
$100	**$150**	**$200**

Cadillac Highway Patrol Car, 20", friction powered, by Ichiko, made in Japan

Good	Excellent	Mint
$375	**$650**	**$875**

Police Department Vehicles

Police Car #8, 10", battery
operated, made in Japan

Good	Excellent	Mint
$50	**$80**	**$135**

Old Sheriff Car, 9 1/2", battery
operated, made in Japan

Good	Excellent	Mint
$90	**$160**	**$200**

Police Car #5, 10", battery
operated, made in Japan

Good	Excellent	Mint
$70	**$140**	**$200**

Police Department Vehicles

'64 Buick Police Car, 11 1/2",
battery operated, by Asakusa,
made in Japan

Good	Excellent	Mint
$100	**$150**	**$200**

'61 Plymouth Highway Patrol
Car, 14", friction powered, by
M, made in Japan

Good	Excellent	Mint
$100	**$150**	**$200**

Lincoln Highway Patrol Car, 11
3/4", friction powered, by
Bandai, made in Japan

Good	Excellent	Mint
$150	**$320**	**$400**

'63 Ford Police Car, 12 1/2",
battery operated, by Taiyo,
made in Japan

Good	Excellent	Mint
$100	**$165**	**$210**

Police Department Vehicles

Buick Riviera Highway Patrol
Car, 11", battery operated, by
Bandai, made in Japan

Good	Excellent	Mint
$60	$85	$110

'58 Chevy Police Car, 5 1/2",
friction powered, made in Japan

Good	Excellent	Mint
$20	$40	$60

Police Patrol Jeep, 17 1/2",
friction powered, by Y, made
in Japan

Good	Excellent	Mint
$170	$260	$350

Police Department Vehicles

Police Car, 6", friction powered wind-up, by K, made in Japan

Good	Excellent	Mint
$75	$115	$145

Police Department Motorcycle, 6 1/4", mechanical, by KD, made in Japan

Good	Excellent	Mint
$100	$175	$220

'63 Chevy Convertible Patrol Car, 13 5/8", by Daiya, made in Japan

Good	Excellent	Mint
$100	$175	$225

'58 Ford Highway Patrol Car, 11", by Modern Toys, made in Japan

Good	Excellent	Mint
$65	$100	$150

Police Department Vehicles

Siren Police Car, 14 1/4",
pressed steel, by Marx,
made in USA

Good	Excellent	Mint
$125	$250	$375

Mercedes Benz 230, 10 1/2",
battery operated, by Bandai,
made in Japan

Good	Excellent	Mint
$110	$165	$190

'61 Buick Police Patrol Car,
16", friction powered, by TN,
made in Japan

Good	Excellent	Mint
$350	$500	$650

'69 Chevy Police Car, 11", by
Alps, made in Japan

Good	Excellent	Mint
$30	$60	$90

Ambulances

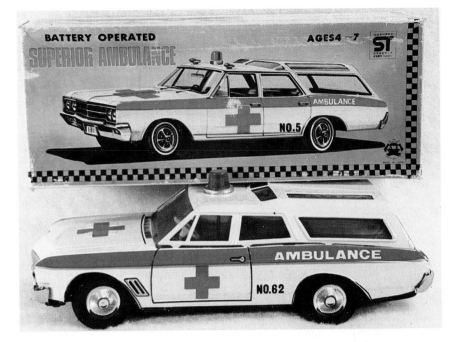

Buick Ambulance, 11 3/4",
battery operated, by Asakusa
Toys, made in Japan

Good	Excellent	Mint
$125	**$225**	**$300**

'62 Rambler Ambulance, 11",
friction powered, by Bandai,
made in Japan

Good	Excellent	Mint
$125	**$200**	**$250**

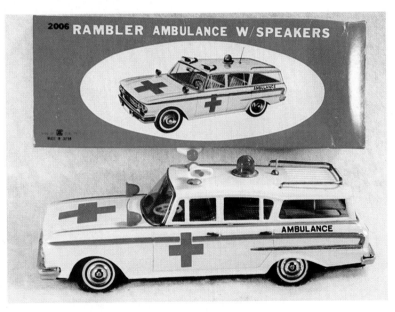

Ambulance, 11 1/4", pressed
steel, by Wyandotte, made in
USA

Good	Excellent	Mint
$100	**$175**	**$225**

Ambulances

'57 Mercury Ambulance, 8 1/4",
friction powered, by Bandai,
made in Japan

Good	Excellent	Mint
$90	$135	$185

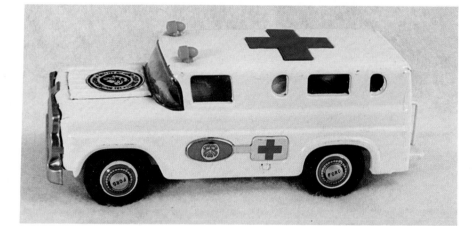

'58 Ford Panel Truck Ambulance, 8 1/2", friction powered,
by Marusan, made in Japan

Good	Excellent	Mint
$85	$135	$175

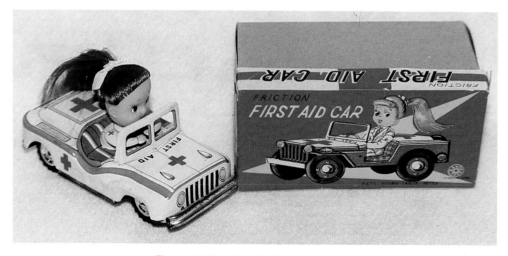

First Aid Car, 5 1/4", friction powered,
by Kanto Toys, made in Japan

Good	Excellent	Mint
$30	$60	$85

Ambulances

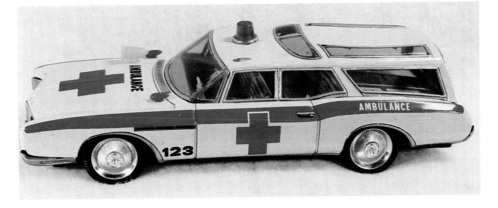

Buick Riviera
Stationwagon Ambulance,
15", friction powered, by
Ashita Toys, made in Japan

Good   Excellent   Mint
$150   **$275**   **$385**

'61 Oldsmobile Ambu-
lance, 12", friction pow-
ered, by Y, made in Japan

Good   Excellent   Mint
$300   **$600**   **$850**

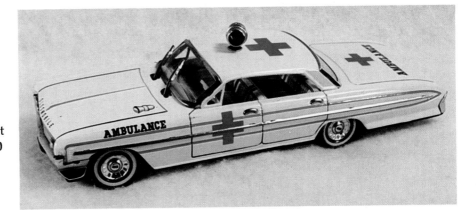

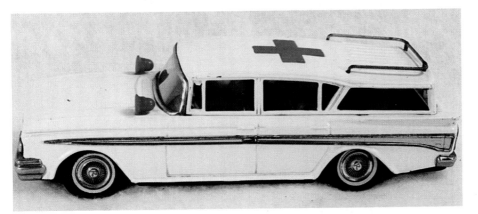

'62 Rambler Ambulance, 11", by
Bandai, made in Japan

Good   Excellent   Mint
$150   **$200**   **$250**

Delivery Trucks

Mack Dump Truck, 20", wind-up,
by Chein, made in USA

Good	Excellent	Mint
$600	$800	$1000

Custom Truck, 14", by
Kubik, made in USA

$500

Pepsi-Cola Truck, 4 1/4", friction
powered, by TT, made in Japan

Good	Excellent	Mint
$150	$200	$250

International Metro Van, 6 1/2",
plastic, by Product Miniature,
made in USA

Good	Excellent	Mint
$75	$160	$250

Delivery Trucks

Dugan's Bakers Truck, 7 1/2",
friction powered, by HTO,
made in Japan

Good	Excellent	Mint
$200	**$400**	**$500**

Grocery Service, 13 1/4", pressed
steel, by Banner, made in USA

Good	Excellent	Mint
$75	**$110**	**$170**

Shell Gasoline Truck, 9 1/4",
friction powered, by San,
made in Japan

Good	Excellent	Mint
$130	**$190**	**$250**

Beer Truck, 3 1/2", diecast,
made in USA

Good	Excellent	Mint
$30	**$40**	**$60**

Delivery Trucks

Fruit Shop Truck, 8 5/8",
friction powered, made in
Japan

Good	Excellent	Mint
$110	**$165**	**$195**

Parcel Service Truck, 12 1/4",
pressed steel, by Structo,
made in USA

Good	Excellent	Mint
$100	**$150**	**$190**

Coca-Cola Truck (Buddy L
custom), 26", by Cowdery,
made in USA

Mint - **$1800**

Delivery Trucks

City Express Truck, 15 3/4",
wind-up, by Buffalo Toys,
made in USA

Good	Excellent	Mint
$170	$250	$350

Consolidated Freight Ways
Truck, 6 1/2", friction pow-
ered, by Mikuni, made in
Japan

Good	Excellent	Mint
$15	$35	$50

Mayflower Truck, 6 1/2", friction
powered, by Mikuni, made in
Japan

Good	Excellent	Mint
$15	$35	$50

Cargo Truck, 14", diecast,
by Smith Miller, made in
USA

Good	Excellent	Mint
$185	$300	$375

Delivery Trucks

Coca-Cola Truck, 10", battery operated, by Taiyo, made in Japan

Good	Excellent	Mint
$70	$90	$135

Repair Truck Step Van, 6 3/4", friction powered, by S, made in Japan

Good	Excellent	Mint
$80	$110	$180

Green Giant Truck, 13 3/4", by Tonka, made in USA

Good	Excellent	Mint
$195	$275	$400

Delivery Trucks

Fanny Farmer Truck, 8 1/2",
made in Japan

Good	Excellent	Mint
$40	$80	$120

Brinks Chevy Truck Bank,
16", by Nylint, made in USA

Good	Excellent	Mint
$30	$65	$100

Jewel Step Van, 8 1/8", made
in Hong Kong

Good	Excellent	Mint
$35	$50	$65

Delivery Trucks

Coca-Cola Truck, 15 1/2",
pressed steel, by Lincoln
Toys, made in Canada

Good	Excellent	Mint
$175	$275	$400

Express Service Truck, 5 5/8",
wind-up, by Triang-Minic,
made in England

Good	Excellent	Mint
$75	$100	$140

Low Bed Dump Truck, 16 1/4",
wind-up, by Gama, made in
Germany

Good	Excellent	Mint
$300	$600	$800

Metalcraft Truck, 11",
pressed steel, by Metalcraft,
made in USA

Good	Excellent	Mint
$200	$350	$500

Delivery Trucks

Custom Truck, 16", by
Lennie, made in USA

$500

Green Giant Co. Truck, 12",
by Tonka, made in USA

Good	Excellent	Mint
$200	**$300**	**$400**

Utility Truck, 12", by Tonka,
made in USA

Good	Excellent	Mint
$90	**$140**	**$175**

Delivery Trucks

City Trucking Co., 21",
pressed steel, by Wyandotte,
made in USA

Good	Excellent	Mint
$100	**$200**	**$300**

Jewel Tea Co. Van, 9 1/2",
made in USA

Good	Excellent	Mint
$85	**$120**	**$160**

Delivery Truck, 15", pressed
steel, by Wyandotte, made
in USA

Good	Excellent	Mint
$90	**$150**	**$250**

'55 Ford Ranchero, 12",
friction powered, by
Bandai, made in Japan

Good	Excellent	Mint
$160	**$240**	**$300**

Delivery Trucks

CW Brand Coffee Truck, 11",
pressed steel, by Metalcraft,
made in USA

Good	Excellent	Mint
$300	$500	$800

Coca-Cola Delivery Truck,
11", pressed steel, by
Metalcraft, made in USA

Good	Excellent	Mint
$350	$700	$1000

Mobil Gas Trucks, 9",
friction powered, by
Bandai, made in Japan

Good	Excellent	Mint
$75	$150	$200

Delivery Truck, 10", pressed
steel, by Wyandotte, made in
USA

Good	Excellent	Mint
$125	$175	$250

Delivery Trucks

Mobil Gas Truck, 9 1/4",
friction powered, by H,
made in Japan

Good	Excellent	Mint
$50	**$85**	**$125**

Custom Truck, 16", by
Lennie, made in USA

$500

Custom Truck, 20
1/2", by Lennie,
made in USA

$500

Delivery Trucks

Mobilgas Truck, 9 1/4",
friction powered, by H,
made in Japan

Good	Excellent	Mint
$50	**$85**	**$125**

Jeep Stake Truck, 7 1/2",
friction powered, by
Bandai, made in Japan

Good	Excellent	Mint
$65	**$125**	**$175**

Old Fashioned Van Truck,
6 1/2", friction powered, by
Bandai, made in Japan

Good	Excellent	Mint
$60	**$100**	**$150**

Delivery Trucks

Express Line Truck, 25",
pressed steel, by Buddy L,
made in USA

Good	Excellent	Mint
$1800	**$2400**	-

Coal Truck, 25", pressed steel,
by Buddy L, made in USA

Good	Excellent	Mint
$2000	**$2600**	-

Nationwide Air Rail Service,
12 3/4", by Wyandotte, made
in USA

Good	Excellent	Mint
$75	**$140**	**$175**

Delivery Trucks

Tanker Truck, 25", pressed steel, by Buddy L, made in USA

Good	Excellent	Mint
$2000	**$2600**	-

Ice Delivery Truck, 26", pressed steel, by Buddy L, made in USA

Good	Excellent	Mint
$1500	**$2200**	-

Sunshine Biscuits Delivery Van, 11 1/2", by Buddy L, made in USA

Good	Excellent	Mint
$100	**$150**	**$200**

Delivery Trucks

Sunshine Fruit Truck with Trailer, 13 1/2", by Marx, made in USA

Good	Excellent	Mint
$75	$140	$185

Coast-to-Coast Stores Delivery Truck, 14 1/2", by Buddy L, made in USA

Good	Excellent	Mint
$90	$175	$230

Pure Ice Delivery Truck, 16", wooden, by Buddy L, made in USA

Good	Excellent	Mint
$90	$140	$185

Toyland Ice Truck, 11 3/4", pressed steel, by Wyandotte, made in USA

Good	Excellent	Mint
$65	$135	$175

Delivery Trucks

Hi Way Express Truck, 16 1/8",
by Marx, made in USA

Good	Excellent	Mint
$60	$125	$200

Read's Truck, 14", by Marx,
made in USA

Good	Excellent	Mint
$110	$165	$190

Curtiss Candy Truck, 9", by
Marx, made in USA

Good	Excellent	Mint
$25	$40	$75

Royal Moving Van, 9 1/2",
wind-up, by Marx, made in
USA

Good	Excellent	Mint
$200	$400	$500

Delivery Trucks

Polar Ice Truck, 14", pressed
steel, by Marx, made in USA

Good	Excellent	Mint
$90	$150	$200

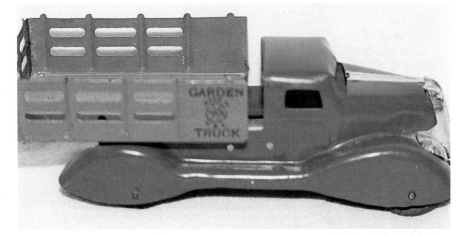

Garden Truck, 10 1/4",
pressed steel, by Marx,
made in USA

Good	Excellent	Mint
$100	$175	$275

Ice Truck, 11", pressed steel, by
Marx, made in USA

Good	Excellent	Mint
$100	$200	$300

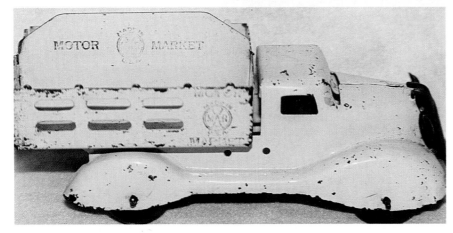

Motor Market Truck, 10 1/2",
pressed steel, by Marx, made
in USA

Good	Excellent	Mint
$100	$200	$300

Delivery Trucks

Railway Express Agency Truck, 20", by Marx, made in USA

Good	Excellent	Mint
$200	**$375**	**$550**

Express Delivery Van, 17 1/2", by Marx, made in Great Britain

Good	Excellent	Mint
$100	**$140**	**$175**

Delivery Trucks

Custom Truck, 21", by Lennie, made in USA

$500

Condor Transcontinental Express,
13", by Marusan, made in Japan

Good	Excellent	Mint
$110	**$185**	**$250**

Public Transportation and Buses

Greyhound Bus, 11 1/2",
friction powered, by
Cragstan, made in Japan

Good	Excellent	Mint
$75	**$100**	**$150**

Greyhound GMC Bus, 8 3/4",
cast iron, by Arcade, made in
USA

Good	Excellent	Mint
$250	**$400**	**$590**

Greyhound Bus Scenicruiser,
10 3/8", friction powered,
made in Japan

Good	Excellent	Mint
$40	**$75**	**$100**

Public Transportation and Buses

Greyhound Bus Scenicruiser, 12 1/2", friction powered, by FTS, made in Japan

Good	Excellent	Mint
$110	**$155**	**$185**

Greyhound Bus, 18", pressed steel wind-up, by Kingsbury, made in USA

Good	Excellent	Mint
$100	**$200**	**$300**

Green Line Bus, 7 1/4", by Triang-Minic Toys, made in England

Good	Excellent	Mint
$110	**$165**	**$220**

Greyhound Bus, 11 1/4", friction powered, made in Japan

Good	Excellent	Mint
$70	**$90**	**$110**

Public Transportation and Buses

Corbett Coach, 11 1/2", friction powered, by MTI, made in China

Good	Excellent	Mint
$5	$20	$30

'63 Continental Trailways Bus, 10 1/2", friction powered, made in Japan

Good	Excellent	Mint
$45	$75	$100

Greyhound Scenicruiser Bus, 10 5/8", by H, made in Japan

Good	Excellent	Mint
$45	$75	$100

Public Transportation and Buses

Greyhound Salt and Pepper Shakers, 3", diecast, made in Japan

Good	Excellent	Mint
$20	**$35**	**$50**

Greyhound Scenicruiser, 11", friction powered, made in Japan

Good	Excellent	Mint
$50	**$75**	**$100**

Greyhound Scenicruiser, 11", by KTS, made in Japan

Good	Excellent	Mint
$50	**$75**	**$100**

Public Transportation and Buses

Greyhound Lines "New York World's Fair", 8 1/4", cast iron, by Arcade, made in USA

Good | Excellent | Mint
$250 | $450 | $700

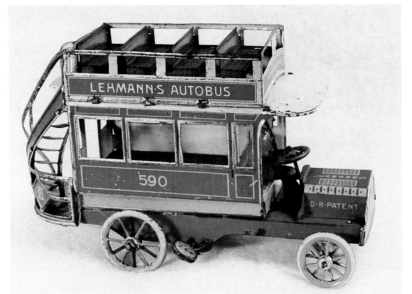

Lehmann's Autobus, 8 1/4", wind-up, by Lehmann, made in Germany

Good | Excellent | Mint
$1100 | $1700 | $2100

Greyhound Express, 3", wind-up, made in Japan

Good | Excellent | Mint
$20 | $35 | $50

Greyhound Lines Bus, 3 1/4", tin, made in USA

Good | Excellent | Mint
$25 | $40 | $50

Public Transportation and Buses

Continental Trailways
Golden Eagle Express, 14",
friction powered, made in
Japan

Good	Excellent	Mint
$40	**$75**	**$100**

Greyhound Bus, 5 5/8", plastic,
battery operated, by Marx, made
in USA

Good	Excellent	Mint
$15	**$30**	**$45**

Greyhound Bus, 6 1/4", friction
powered, by SSS, made in Japan

Good	Excellent	Mint
$40	**$70**	**$90**

Greyhound Bus, 7", diecast,
by Tootsietoy, made in USA

Good	Excellent	Mint
$20	**$35**	**$50**

Public Transportation and Buses

Greyhound Bus, 5 3/4",
diecast, by Tootsietoy, made
in USA

Good	Excellent	Mint
$40	**$55**	**$90**

Greyhound Bus, 18", friction
powered, by Y, made in Japan

Good	Excellent	Mint
$125	**$225**	**$350**

Greyhound, 5", diecast, by
Tootsietoy, made in USA

Good	Excellent	Mint
$5	**$10**	**$15**

Greyhound Lines Bus, 11 1/2",
by Y, made in Japan

Good	Excellent	Mint
$80	**$100**	**$150**

Public Transportation and Buses

Greyhound Bus, 6", diecast, by Tootsietoy, made in USA

Good   Excellent   Mint
$30   **$45**   **$55**

Bonnet Bus, 10", wind-up, by Guntherman

Good   Excellent   Mint
$150   **$250**   **$325**

Greyhound Scenicruiser, 10", made in Japan

Good   Excellent   Mint
$90   **$100**   **$135**

Greyhound Bus, 9 1/4", diecast, by Realistic, made in USA

Good   Excellent   Mint
$80   **$100**   **$150**

Public Transportation and Buses

School Bus, 10 1/4", battery operated, by Alps, made in Japan

Good	Excellent	Mint
$40	**$80**	**$120**

School Bus, 13 1/2", battery operated, by Daiya, made in Japan

Good	Excellent	Mint
$120	**$175**	**$235**

American Airlines Shuttle Truck, 8 1/2", friction powered, by H, made in Japan

Good	Excellent	Mint
$60	**$95**	**$125**

Public Transportation and Buses

Greyhound Bus Salt & Pepper Shakers, 3 1/8", diecast, made in Japan

Good	Excellent	Mint
$20	$35	$50

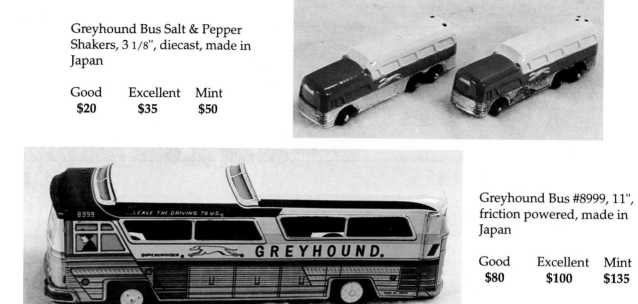

Greyhound Bus #8999, 11", friction powered, made in Japan

Good	Excellent	Mint
$80	$100	$135

Around the World Bus, 13 1/4", friction powered, by Daiya, made in Japan

Good	Excellent	Mint
$300	$400	$550

Greyhound Scenicruiser, 11 1/4", friction powered, by TN, made in Japan

Good	Excellent	Mint
$110	$155	$220

School Bus, 12", battery operated, made in Japan

Good	Excellent	Mint
$85	$120	$160

Public Transportation and Buses

Greyhound Bus, 8", by Corgi, made in China

New
$35

School Bus, 11 1/2", friction powered, by Daito, made in Japan

Good	Excellent	Mint
$110	**$150**	**$220**

Greyhound Scenicruiser, 11 3/4", friction powered, by HTC, made in Japan

Good	Excellent	Mint
$110	**$155**	**$200**

Public Transportation and Buses

Touring Bus, 15 1/2", friction powered, by Joustra, made in France

Good	Excellent	Mint
$110	**$175**	**$225**

Greyhound Bus, 11", friction powered, by KTS, made in Japan

Good	Excellent	Mint
$80	**$100**	**$150**

Panda Bear Bus, 16", friction powered, by TM, made in Japan

Good	Excellent	Mint
$100	**$165**	**$225**

Public Transportation and Buses

Bus, 16 1/2", by Asakusa, friction powered, made in Japan

Good	Excellent	Mint
$190	**$250**	**$350**

Trailways Bus, 9 1/2", diecast, by Realistic, made in USA

Good	Excellent	Mint
$80	**$150**	**$200**

Greyhound Bus, 15", friction powered, made in Japan

Good	Excellent	Mint
$60	**$120**	**$175**

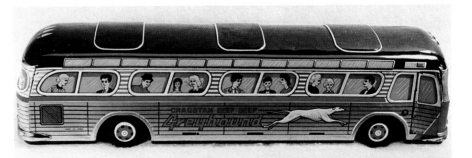

Greyhound Bus with Opening Door, 20 1/2", friction powered, made in Japan

Good	Excellent	Mint
$100	**$200**	**$300**

Public Transportation and Buses

Greyhound Bus, 18", wind-up, by Kingsbury, made in USA

Good	Excellent	Mint
$200	**$375**	**$550**

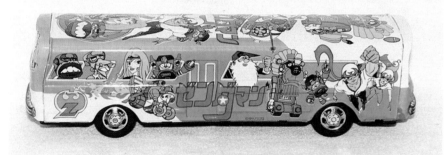

Japanese Cartoon Bus, 14", by TT, made in Japan

Good	Excellent	Mint
$90	**$175**	**$275**

Greyhound Bus, 11", friction powered, made in Japan

Good	Excellent	Mint
$75	**$130**	**$160**

Panoramic Overland Bus, 12 3/4", friction powered, by H, made in Japan

Good	Excellent	Mint
$200	**$300**	**$400**

Tow Trucks

Wreck Truck, 11 1/4", friction powered, made in Japan

Good	Excellent	Mint
$50	$85	$110

Wrecker, 16 1/2", by Buddy L, made in USA

Good	Excellent	Mint
$110	$190	$225

Wrecker Towing Truck, 12", by Marx, made in USA

Good	Excellent	Mint
$65	$100	$150

Tow Trucks

Wrecker, 22", pressed steel,
made in USA

Good	Excellent	Mint
$110	**$175**	**$210**

Wrecker, 6", friction powered,
made in Japan

Good	Excellent	Mint
$25	**$50**	**$100**

Wrecker, 5 1/2", friction powered, by Marx, made in Japan

Good	Excellent	Mint
$50	**$85**	**$110**

Ford Wrecker, 13 1/2", friction
powered, made in Japan

Good	Excellent	Mint
$85	**$100**	**$150**

Tow Trucks

Wrecker, 12", pressed steel,
by Structo, made in USA

Good	Excellent	Mint
$100	$150	$185

Wrecker, 15 1/2", plastic
and pressed steel, by
Wyandotte, made in USA

Good	Excellent	Mint
$60	$100	$125

Wrecker, 20", pressed steel,
by Triang, made in England

Good	Excellent	Mint
$200	$390	$490

Tow Trucks

Wrecker, 13", pressed steel, by Wyandotte, made in USA

Good	Excellent	Mint
$110	**$175**	**$210**

Wrecker, 11 1/2", pressed steel, made in USA

Good	Excellent	Mint
$100	**$150**	**$185**

GMC Service Wrecker, 10", friction powered, made in Japan

Good	Excellent	Mint
$75	**$100**	**$150**

Nite and Day Wrecker, 21", by Marx, made in USA

Good	Excellent	Mint
$100	**$155**	**$200**

Tow Trucks

Wrecker, 13", pressed steel,
by Metalcraft, made in USA

Good	Excellent	Mint
$160	$225	$350

Wrecker, 20", pressed steel,
by Schieble, made in USA

Good	Excellent	Mint
$180	$375	$475

Wrecker, 28", pressed steel,
by Buddy L, made in USA

Good	Excellent	Mint
$135	$195	$325

Cities Service Wrecker, 20",
by Marx, made in USA

Good	Excellent	Mint
$150	$250	$300

Tow Trucks

Wrecker, 15", pressed steel, by Buddy L, made in USA

Good	Excellent	Mint
$80	**$120**	**$160**

Jeep Wrecker, 16", by Marx, made in USA

Good	Excellent	Mint
$90	**$150**	**$200**

Ford Tow Truck with '60 Chevy Impala, 10" and 7 1/2", friction powered, by Ichiko, made in Japan

Good	Excellent	Mint
$125	**$250**	**$375**

Tow Trucks

Wrecker, 11 1/2", pressed steel, by Metalcraft, made in USA

Good	Excellent	Mint
$150	**$250**	**$300**

Wrecker, 13", pressed steel, by Metalcraft, made in USA

Good	Excellent	Mint
$170	**$250**	**$385**

Wrecker Tow Truck, 16 1/2", pressed steel, by Lincoln Toys, made in Canada

Good	Excellent	Mint
$75	**$175**	**$250**

Tow Truck, 22 1/2", pressed steel, by Structo, made in USA

Good	Excellent	Mint
$100	**$175**	**$230**

Tow Trucks

Wrecker, 12 1/2", by Hubley,
made in USA

Good	Excellent	Mint
$65	$110	$135

Wrecker, 16", diecast, by
Smith Miller, made in USA

Custom
$700

Wrecker, 9 3/8", wind-up, by
Marx, made in USA

Good	Excellent	Mint
$150	$300	$475

Tow Trucks

Wrecker, 13", wind-up, by
Mettoy, made in Great Britain

Good	Excellent	Mint
$110	**$220**	**$300**

Wrecker, 10", by Tonka,
made in USA

Good	Excellent	Mint
$110	**$150**	**$200**

Wrecker, 13", pressed steel,
by Richmond Toys, made in
USA

Good	Excellent	Mint
$150	**$200**	**$250**

Tow Trucks

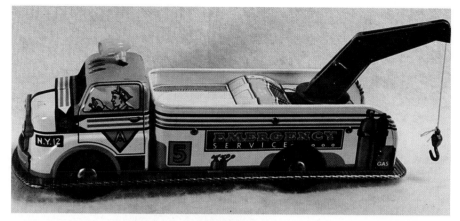

Wrecker Emergency Service,
15 3/4", friction powered, by
Marx, made in USA

Good	Excellent	Mint
$100	$150	$225

Wrecker, 10 1/2", diecast,
made in USA

Good	Excellent	Mint
$75	$100	$150

Wrecker, 6 1/4", plastic, by
Hubley, made in USA

Good	Excellent	Mint
$30	$60	$95

Wrecker, 12", pressed steel,
made in USA

Good	Excellent	Mint
$90	$150	$200

Tow Trucks

Wrecker, 7 1/4", diecast, by
Hubley, made in USA

Good	Excellent	Mint
$65	**$110**	**$140**

Wrecker, 14 3/4", diecast and
metal, by Smith Miller, made
in USA

Good	Excellent	Mint
$200	**$250**	**$325**

Wrecker, 14", aluminum, by
Merri Toy, made in USA

Good	Excellent	Mint
$75	**$100**	**$125**

Wrecker, 13", pressed steel,
by Structo, made in USA

Good	Excellent	Mint
$50	**$90**	**$130**

Tow Trucks

Tandem Wrecker, 24", by Buddy L, made in USA

Good	Excellent	Mint
$100	$200	$300

Ford Wrecker, 15", friction powered, by Linemar, made in Japan

Good	Excellent	Mint
$140	$200	$265

Wrecker and Taxi, 14",
aluminum, by Merri Toy,
made in USA

Good	Excellent	Mint
$75	$100	$125

Tow Trucks

Wrecker, 12", pressed steel, by Marx, made in USA

Good	Excellent	Mint
$150	**$225**	**$275**

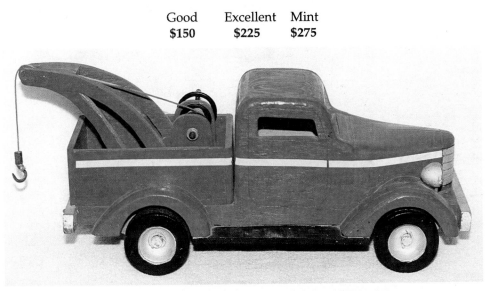

Custom Wrecker, 16", wooden, made in USA

Good	Excellent	Mint
$35	**$75**	**$125**

Custom Truck, 12", by Lennie, made in USA

$300

Dump Trucks

Ford F800 Dump Truck, 11 1/4",
friction powered, by ATC,
made in Japan

Good	Excellent	Mint
$80	**$110**	**$140**

'60 Chevy Dump Truck, 9", by
ATC, made in Japan

Good	Excellent	Mint
$75	**$100**	**$140**

Sand and Gravel Truck, 9 1/2",
wind-up, made in USA

Good	Excellent	Mint
$280	**$450**	**$550**

Dump Trucks

Chevy Dump Truck, 19 1/2", by Marx, made in USA

Good	Excellent	Mint
$100	**$165**	**$210**

'60 Ford Dump Truck, 15 1/2", friction
powered, by SE, made in Japan

Good	Excellent	Mint
$100	**$150**	**$185**

Dump Trucks

Truck, 21 1/2", pressed steel,
by Structo, made in USA

Good	Excellent	Mint
$150	**$225**	**$275**

White Dump Truck, 25",
pressed steel, by JC Penney,
made in USA

Good	Excellent	Mint
$250	**$450**	-

Mack Dump Truck, 23",
pressed steel, by Boy Craft,
made in USA

Good	Excellent	Mint
$290	**$400**	-

Dump Truck, 15 1/2", pressed
steel, made in USA

Good	Excellent	Mint
$125	**$200**	**$375**

Dump Trucks

Side Dump Trailer, 9",
friction powered, by
Cragstan, made in Japan

Good	Excellent	Mint
$30	$65	$100

Chevy Dump Truck, 10 3/4",
friction powered, by TN,
made in Japan

Good	Excellent	Mint
$65	$100	$140

Isuzu Dump Truck, 9 1/4",
friction powered, by ATC,
made in Japan

Good	Excellent	Mint
$70	$110	$140

Dump Trucks

'57 Studebaker Dump Truck, 18", by Marx, made in USA

Good	Excellent	Mint
$125	**$165**	**$225**

Dump Truck, 11 3/4", aluminum, by Merri Toy, made in USA

Good	Excellent	Mint
$30	**$60**	**$100**

Dump Truck, 15 3/4", pressed steel, made in USA

Good	Excellent	Mint
$250	**$350**	-

Mighty Metal Dump Truck, 11 1/2", by Hubley, made in USA

Good	Excellent	Mint
$45	**$85**	**$110**

Dump Trucks

Dump Truck, 27 1/2", pressed steel, by Turner, made in USA

Good	Excellent	Mint
$100	$160	$220

Glen Dale Coal Co. Truck, 12 3/8", by Marx, made in USA

Good	Excellent	Mint
$70	$140	$200

Sand and Gravel Truck, 10 1/2", pressed steel, by Marx, made in USA

Good	Excellent	Mint
$115	$200	$250

Dump Truck, 19 1/2", by Chein, made in USA

Good	Excellent	Mint
$300	$500	$650

Livestock Trucks

Horse Van, 5 3/4", friction
powered, made in Japan

Good	Excellent	Mint
$50	$70	$95

'20's Animal Truck, 6", tin

Good	Excellent	Mint
$75	$125	$175

Animal Van Truck, 9", friction
powered, made in Japan

Good	Excellent	Mint
$80	$110	$165

Lazy Day Farms, 17 1/2", pressed
steel, by Marx, made in USA

Good	Excellent	Mint
$100	$200	$300

Cement Mixer Trucks

Ready Mix Truck, 17",
pressed steel, by Structo,
made in USA

Good   Excellent   Mint
$55   **$85**   **$120**

Cement Mixer, 14 3/8",
friction powered, made in
Japan

Good   Excellent   Mint
$40   **$70**   **$110**

Jeep Cement Mixer, 10 3/4",
friction powered, by TN, made
in Japan

Good   Excellent   Mint
$90   **$140**   **$175**

Cement Mixer Trucks

Cement Mixer, 13 3/4",
friction powered, by
Cragstan, made in Japan

Good   Excellent   Mint
$80   **$140**   **$200**

Gravel Mixer, 10 1/4",
pressed steel, by Marx,
made in USA

Good   Excellent   Mint
$125   **$175**   **$300**

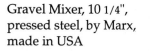

Ready Mix Truck, 15 1/2",
pressed steel, by Structo,
made in USA

Good   Excellent   Mint
$55   **$85**   **$120**

Cement Mixer Trucks

International Cement Mixer, 10 1/2", battery operated, by Modern Toys, made in Japan

Good	Excellent	Mint
$90	**$140**	**$185**

Super Concrete Mixer, 12", friction powered, by Toymaster, made in Japan

Good	Excellent	Mint
$90	**$140**	**$185**

Ready Mix Truck, 22", pressed steel, by Structo, made in USA

Good	Excellent	Mint
$90	**$125**	**$150**

Truck Transports

Auto Transport, 15", battery operated, by Linemar, made in Japan

Good	Excellent	Mint
$115	$145	$175

Speedway Racing Transport, 23 1/2", friction powered, by Sears, made in Japan

Good	Excellent	Mint
$210	$300	$400

Truck Transports

Car Carrier with Turbo Power, 27 1/2", by Nylint, made in USA

Good	Excellent	Mint
$80	$100	$150

Chitwood Thrill Show Carrier, 21" box, by Ertl, made in USA

with box **$125**

Speedway Truck, 19", pressed steel, by Buddy L, made in USA

Good	Excellent	Mint
$275	$400	$600

Truck Transports

Car Carrier #840, 28 1/2",
by Tonka, made in USA

Good	Excellent	Mint
$90	$130	$185

Truck Transport, 25",
pressed steel, by Lincoln,
made in Canada

Good	Excellent	Mint
$200	$300	$600

Smith Miller Custom
Car Carrier, 39", made
in USA (carrier), made
in China (Corvettes)

Custom **$1200**

Auto Transport, 14 1/2", by
Marx, made in USA

Good	Excellent	Mint
$30	$50	$75

Truck Transports

Auto Transport, by Hubley, made in USA

Good	Excellent	Mint
$40	$50	$75

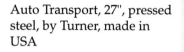

Auto Transport, 27", pressed steel, by Turner, made in USA

Good	Excellent	Mint
$200	$350	$475

Auto Transport, 22 1/2", pressed steel, by Girard, made in USA

Good	Excellent	Mint
$250	$400	$500

Speedway Transport, 18 1/2", by Buddy L, made in USA

Good	Excellent	Mint
$275	$400	$600

Truck Transports

Auto Transport, 22", by
Marx, made in USA

Good	Excellent	Mint
$150	**$220**	**$300**

Car Transport, 23 1/4",
friction powered, made in
Japan

Good	Excellent	Mint
$185	**$250**	**$300**

Car Carrier, 9 1/4", by Tonka,
made in USA

Good	Excellent	Mint
$20	**$40**	**$65**

Miscellaneous Trucks

Machinery Hauler, 18",
pressed steel, made in USA

Good	Excellent	Mint
$110	$185	$275

Magnetic Crane, 18",
pressed steel, made in USA

Good	Excellent	Mint
$170	$250	$300

Easter Truck, 7 1/2", made in
USA

Good	Excellent	Mint
$150	$200	$250

Miscellaneous Trucks

Pan American Starter Truck
#P3, 3 3/4", made in Japan

Good	Excellent	Mint
$80	$120	$170

IHC Pickup, 8", friction
powered, by Bandai, made
in Japan

Good	Excellent	Mint
$85	$140	$175

Ford Ramp Truck, 19", by Tonka, made in USA

Good	Excellent	Mint
$350	$550	$700

Miscellaneous Trucks

Garbage Truck, 13 1/4",
pressed steel, by Marx,
made in USA

Good	Excellent	Mint
$100	$185	$225

Ford Truck, 19", friction powered, made in Japan

Good	Excellent	Mint
$400	$850	$1200

Friction Truck #52, 10 1/4", by
American Toys, made in USA

Good	Excellent	Mint
$150	$250	$350

Miscellaneous Trucks

Prewar Truck, 6 3/4", made in Japan

Good	Excellent	Mint
$80	$165	$250

'58 Ford Ranchero, 7 3/4", friction powered, by Bandai, made in Japan

Good	Excellent	Mint
$80	$110	$165

G.B.C. Pickup, 7", battery operated, by ATC, made in Japan

Good	Excellent	Mint
$50	$85	$125

Miscellaneous Trucks

Machinery Hauling Truck,
14 1/2", pressed steel, by
Metalcraft, made in USA

Good   Excellent   Mint
$450   **$700**   **$1400**

Machinery Hauling Truck,
14 ", pressed steel, by
Metalcraft, made in USA

Good   Excellent   Mint
$450   **$650**   **$1300**

Bell Telephone Truck, 14"
without pole, by Hubley,
made in USA

Good   Excellent   Mint
$490   **$800**   **$950**

Miscellaneous Trucks

Piledriver Truck, 12 3/4", by Hubley,
made in USA (two views shown)

Good	Excellent	Mint
$65	$110	$150

P.I.E. Truck, 8 3/4", friction powered, made in Japan

Good	Excellent	Mint
$70	$100	$130

Miscellaneous Semis

White Freightliner Semi, 16",
made in Japan

Good	Excellent	Mint
$70	**$110**	**$140**

Bekins Double Van Trailer,
15 3/4", friction powered,
by Linemar, made in Japan

Good	Excellent	Mint
$150	**$250**	**$350**

Colonial Trailer Semi, 12 1/2",
friction powered, made in
Japan

Good	Excellent	Mint
$125	**$240**	**$280**

Miscellaneous Semis

Gerard Motor Express, 9", by
Tootsietoy, made in USA

Good	Excellent	Mint
$65	$85	$120

Fast Freight Semi, 8 7/8",
friction powered, made in
Japan

Good	Excellent	Mint
$45	$70	$125

Murphy Freight Semi, 21 1/2",
friction powered, made in
Japan

Good	Excellent	Mint
$75	$120	$200

Ace Semi, 22 1/4", by
Lumar, made in USA

Good	Excellent	Mint
$80	$135	$200

Miscellaneous Semis

Mayflower Movers, 8 1/2",
by Ralstoy, made in USA

Good	Excellent	Mint
$25	$50	$70

Marshall Field and Co., 22",
by Tonka, made in USA

Good	Excellent	Mint
$350	$700	$950

Lumar Lines, 26 3/4", by
Lumar

Good	Excellent	Mint
$160	$200	$250

Timberking Log Hauler, 18 1/2",
wind-up, by Strauss, made
in USA

Good	Excellent	Mint
$375	$700	$1000

Miscellaneous Semis

Log Hauler, 17 1/2", diecast, by Hubley, made in USA

Good	Excellent	Mint
$40	$75	$110

Smith Miller Lowboy, 26", diecast, by Smith Miller, made in USA

Good	Excellent	Mint
$150	$220	$275

Lyon Van Lines, 21 1/2", by Smith Miller, made in USA

Good	Excellent	Mint
$400	$600	$700

White's Semi, 25", pressed steel, by Lumar, made in Japan

Good	Excellent	Mint
$150	$250	$350

Miscellaneous Semis

Morton Salt Ford Semi, 12 3/8",
friction powered, made in Japan

Good	Excellent	Mint
$110	**$200**	**$275**

White Freightliner for
Transcon Lines, 21 1/2",
friction powered, made in
Japan

Good	Excellent	Mint
$160	**$210**	**$275**

Consolidated Freightways,
21 3/4", friction powered,
made in Japan

Good	Excellent	Mint
$100	**$150**	**$200**

Miscellaneous Semis

Mack P.I.E. Truck, 28 3/4", by Smith Miller, made in USA

Good	Excellent	Mint
$400	$600	$850

Ellis Foods Tractor and Trailer, 13", friction powered, by Linemar, made in Japan

Good	Excellent	Mint
$100	$150	$200

Pan Am Clipper Cargo Truck, 8 1/2", by Ralstoy, made in USA

Good	Excellent	Mint
$20	$45	$65

Atlas Van-Lines, 8 1/2", by Ralstoy, made in USA

Good	Excellent	Mint
$30	$40	$55

Miscellaneous Semis

Grain Hauler, 9", friction powered, made in Japan

Good	Excellent	Mint
$30	$65	$100

GMC Rexall Drug Tractor and Trailer, 26", friction powered, made in Japan

Good	Excellent	Mint
$200	$300	$390

Hill Security Van Lines, 8 1/2", by Ralstoy, made in USA

Good	Excellent	Mint
$30	$40	$55

Miscellaneous Semis

U.S. Mail Semi, 8 1/2", by
Ralstoy, made in USA

Good	Excellent	Mint
$30	**$40**	**$55**

Hoerner Waldorf Corp., 8 1/2",
by Ralstoy, made in USA

Good	Excellent	Mint
$30	**$40**	**$55**

Wheaton Semi, 8 1/2", by
Ralstoy, made in USA

Good	Excellent	Mint
$30	**$40**	**$55**

Red Ball Semi, 8 1/2", by
Ralstoy, made in USA

Good	Excellent	Mint
$30	**$40**	**$55**

Miscellaneous Semis

GMC Gold Bond Semi, 17",
friction powered, by SSS,
made in Japan

Good	Excellent	Mint
$150	**$225**	**$300**

Tank Trailer Truck, 12", by
M, made in Japan

Good	Excellent	Mint
$50	**$90**	**$120**

Sears Van Trailer, 16", made
in Japan

Good	Excellent	Mint
$85	**$135**	**$175**

Miscellaneous Semis

Canadian Pacific Express, 21 1/2", friction powered, made in Japan

Good	Excellent	Mint
$150	**$250**	**$350**

Chicago Stockyard and American Can Co. Trucks, 3 3/4", friction powered, made in Japan

Good	Excellent	Mint
$30	**$50**	**$85**

Express Truck, 20 1/4", by Kingsbury, made in USA

Good	Excellent	Mint
$160	**$240**	**$335**

ABC Freight Semi, 11 1/2", friction powered, by K, made in Japan

Good	Excellent	Mint
$60	**$100**	**$150**

200

Ice Cream and Dairy Trucks

Ice Cream Van, 4 1/4", friction powered, made in Japan

Good   Excellent   Mint
$60   **$80**   **$100**

Mister Softee Van, 4 1/4", friction powered, made in Japan

Good   Excellent   Mint
$60   **$80**   **$100**

Good Humor Hot Wheel Vans, 2 3/4", by Mattel, made in Japan

Mint - **$10**

Milk Delivery Van, 6 1/2", friction powered, by MSK, made in Japan

Good   Excellent   Mint
$50   **$100**   **$150**

Ice Cream and Dairy Trucks

Dodge Milk Truck, 8 1/2",
friction powered, by M,
made in Japan

Good	Excellent	Mint
$65	**$100**	**$150**

Milk Tank Truck, 9 1/4", by
H, made in Japan

Good	Excellent	Mint
$40	**$75**	**$100**

Fresh Milk Truck, 7 1/4",
friction powered, by Yone,
made in Japan

Good	Excellent	Mint
$30	**$60**	**$90**

Fresh Milk Delivery, 5 3/4",
friction powered, made in
Japan

Good	Excellent	Mint
$35	**$65**	**$95**

Ice Cream and Dairy Trucks

Carnation Milk Delivery Van, 12", by Tonka, made in USA

Good	Excellent	Mint
$225	**$390**	**$475**

Dodge Ice Cream Truck, 8 1/2", friction powered, by M, made in Japan

Good	Excellent	Mint
$110	**$165**	**$195**

Big Wheel Ice Cream Truck, 10 1/4", battery operated, by Taiyo, made in Japan

Good	Excellent	Mint
$80	**$100**	**$130**

Ice Cream and Dairy Trucks

Home Dairy Truck, 12", plastic cab with metal bed, by Marx, made in USA

Good	Excellent	Mint
$45	$85	$120

Ice Cream Truck, 5 3/4", friction powered, made in Japan

Good	Excellent	Mint
$70	$100	$125

Arden Milk and Ice Cream Truck, 13 1/2", diecast and wooden, by Smith Miller, made in USA

Good	Excellent	Mint
$200	$300	$400

Ice Cream Truck, 3 1/2", friction powered, made in Japan

Good	Excellent	Mint
$15	$30	$45

Ice Cream and Dairy Trucks

Ice Cream Van, 7", friction
powered, made in Japan

Good   Excellent   Mint
$70 $110 $165

Howard Johnson's Truck, 9 1/2",
plastic, by Marx, made in USA

Good   Excellent   Mint
$75 $100 $150

Ice Cream Vendor Truck, 7",
friction powered, by KO,
made in Japan

Good   Excellent   Mint
$100 $160 $200

Ice Cream Truck, 8 1/2", wind-
up, by Courtland, made in
USA

Good   Excellent   Mint
$100 $150 $200

Ice Cream and Dairy Trucks

Ice Cream Van, 11 3/8", by Buddy L, made in USA

Good	Excellent	Mint
$90	$150	$200

Ice Cream Truck, 2 1/4", made in China

Mint - $5

Ice Cream Truck, 2", made in Taiwan

Good	Excellent	Mint
$20	$35	$45

Ice Cream Truck, 7 1/2", friction powered, made in Japan

Good	Excellent	Mint
$50	$100	$150

Tractors and Heavy Machinery

Early Farm Toys, by
Minneapolis Moline, made
in USA

Tractor, 5 1/2"

Good	Excellent	Mint
$165	$275	$350

Spreader, 7 1/4"

Good	Excellent	Mint
$110	$200	$250

Disc Harrow, 8 1/4"

Good	Excellent	Mint
$110	$200	$250

Road Sweeper, 4", friction
powered, by Yamaich,
made in Japan

Good	Excellent	Mint
$30	$60	$80

Conveyancer Fork Lift, 10",
battery operated, by Owen,
made in England

Good	Excellent	Mint
$140	$170	$225

Tractors and Heavy Machinery

Fork Lift, 5 1/2", friction powered, by Linemar, made in Japan

Good	Excellent	Mint
$40	$75	$100

Golf Club Tractor, 11 1/2", by Tonka, made in USA

Good	Excellent	Mint
$80	$150	$225

Little Jim Tractor and Trailer, 12", wind-up, by Kingsbury, made in USA

Good	Excellent	Mint
$175	$300	$450

Tractors and Heavy Machinery

'20 Dozer, 8 1/4", wind-up, by Structo, made in USA

Good	Excellent	Mint
$150	**$250**	**$350**

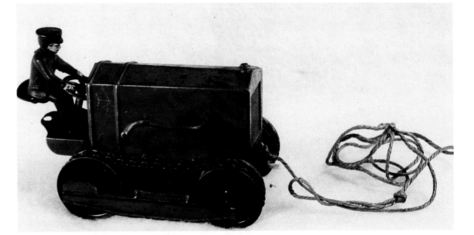

Cat, 7 3/4", wind-up, by Kingsbury

Good	Excellent	Mint
$165	**$250**	**$325**

'21 Cat, 8 1/2", wind-up, by Structo, made in USA

Good	Excellent	Mint
$195	**$290**	**$365**

Tractors and Heavy Machinery

Fork Lift, 8", by Modern Toys, made in Japan

Good	Excellent	Mint
$70	**$110**	**$150**

Bulldozer, 9 1/2", battery operated, by TN, made in Japan

Good	Excellent	Mint
$60	**$90**	**$140**

Jeeps and Dune Buggies

Surrey Jeep, 6 3/4", tin, friction powered, made in Japan

Good	Excellent	Mint
$60	$100	$140

Willys Jeep, 10 1/2", diecast, made in USA

Good	Excellent	Mint
$75	$125	$175

Dune Buggy, 12 1/2", gas powered, by L.M. Cox, made in USA

Good	Excellent	Mint
$45	$80	$120

Jeeps and Dune Buggies

Dune Buggy, 9 3/4", battery operated, by Alps, made in Japan

Good	Excellent	Mint
$50	$80	$125

Jeepster, 10", battery operated, by Daiya, made in Japan

Good	Excellent	Mint
$60	$100	$125

Animal Jeep, 5 1/4", friction powered, by Daiya, made in Japan

Good	Excellent	Mint
$20	$30	$50

Jeeps and Dune Buggies

Surrey Jeep, 11", battery operated, by TN, made in Japan

Good	Excellent	Mint
$65	$85	$150

Surrey Jeep, 6", diecast, made in USA

Good	Excellent	Mint
$85	$110	$160

Fix-All Jeep, 7 1/2", by Marx, made in USA

Good	Excellent	Mint
$60	$130	$250

Gas Station Sets

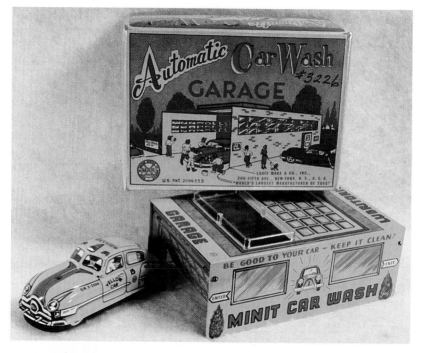

Automatic Wash Garage, 9",
cab- 6 1/2", wind-up, by
Marx, made in USA

Good   Excellent   Mint
$100   **$200**   **$275**

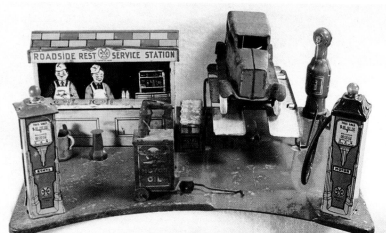

Roadside Rest Service
Station, 13 3/4", by Marx,
made in USA

Good   Excellent   Mint
$300   **$400**   **$500**

Shell Service Penny Toy, 4",
made in Germany

Good   Excellent   Mint
$160   **$200**   **$300**

Shell Station Penny Toy, 4",
made in Germany

Good   Excellent   Mint
$300   **$400**   **$500**

Gas Station Sets

Honeymoon Garage, 7", cars- 6",
by Marx, made in USA

Good	Excellent	Mint
$125	**$200**	**$300**

Mobilgas Service Station, 10",
cars- 3 1/4", wind-up, made
in Japan

Good	Excellent	Mint
$125	**$180**	**$220**

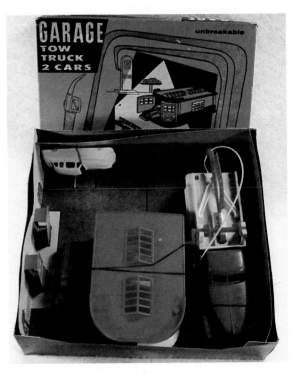

Service Station Penny Toy,
2 7/8", made in Germany

Good	Excellent	Mint
$120	**$140**	**$180**

Garage Set, by Payton Products, made in USA

Mint with box - **$190**

Gas Station Sets

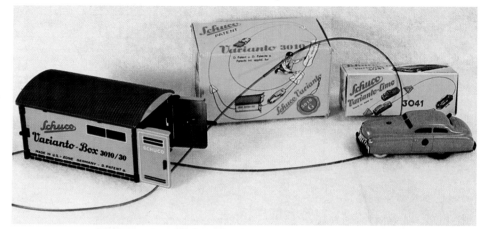

Varianto Garage and Limousine, 4 3/4", limo- 4 1/4", by Schuco, made in Germany

Good	Excellent	Mint
$85	**$140**	**$200**

Gas Station, 9 1/2", cars- 4 1/2", friction powered, by Y, made in Japan

Good	Excellent	Mint
$130	**$180**	**$250**

Garages, 4", cars- 3", made in West Germany

Good	Excellent	Mint
$100	**$175**	**$275**

Garage and Truck, 13", truck- 10", pressed steel, by Metalcraft, made in USA

Garage
Good	Excellent	Mint
$75	**$100**	**$150**

Truck
Good	Excellent	Mint
$100	**$200**	**$300**

Car Sets and Toy Displays

Gulf Wood Blocks Gas Station
Set, 11", made in West Germany

Set with Box: **$190**

Racing Car Presentation set with
Box, 5" cars, by Triang-Minic,
made in England

Good	Excellent	Mint
$250	**$450**	**$800**

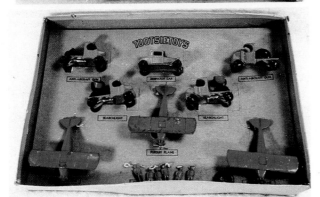

Aerial Defense Set #5061 with Box, 15"
box, by Tootsietoy, made in USA

Good	Excellent	Mint
$650	**$900**	**$1400**

Car Sets and Toy Displays

Hot Rods, 5", plastic, by E-Line, made in USA

Good	Excellent	Mint
$10	**$15**	**$40**

Volkswagen 1300 Display, 5 1/4", friction powered, made in Japan

Complete- **$325**

Kar-Kit Set, 10 1/2", by Toy Founders, made in USA

Good	Excellent	Mint
$75	**$200**	**$300**

Car Sets and Toy Displays

Mini-Hi-Way Racing Car Gift Set with Box, 7", diecast, by Triang, made in England

Mint Boxed Set: **$350**

Keystone Traffic Outfit, 12 1/2" box, made in USA

Set with Box- **$185**

Antique Vehicles Gift Set, 13" box, friction powered, by SSS, made in Japan

Complete Set- **$325**

Car Sets and Toy Displays

6 Racing Machine Series in Display Box, 5"
cars, friction powered, by Y, made in Japan

Set with Box- **$400**

'59 Ford Convertible Drive Set,
6", by TM, made in Japan

Set with Box- **$275**

Tour De France Gift Set, 9", by Corgi

Set with Box- **$160**

Car Sets and Toy Displays

'58 Lincoln Set, 5 3/4" cars, by Sanyo, made in Japan

Set with Box- **$165**

Tootsietoy Fire Dept. #5211, 13" box, by Tootsietoy, made in USA

Mint Set with Box- **$550**

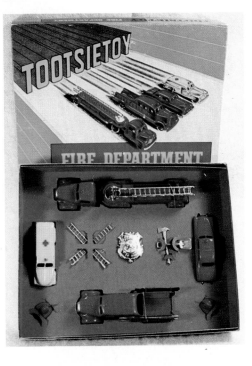

Structo Cub Set, 11 1/4", by Structo, made in USA

Good	Excellent	Mint
$110	**$175**	**$250**

Three Car Set, 11", by Built Rite Toys, made in USA

Mint with Box- **$125**

Car Sets and Toy Displays

Steam Engine and Accessories, 9 1/4" box, by Marx, made in Japan

Complete Set- **$325**

Indianapolis Speed Race, 7 1/4" package, spring action, by Thomas Mfg. Corp., made in USA

Set with Package- **$65**

Tootsietoy Speedway, 15", by Tootsietoy, made in USA

Set with Box- **$2500**

Indy 500 Combo Kit, 12 1/2", by AMT

Mint in Box- **$100**

Truck Sets

Trailer Fleet #675-5, by Tonka, made in USA

Mint Set with Box- **$1800**

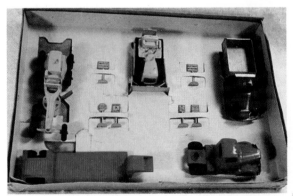

Road Construction Assortment, 16" box, by Tootsietoy, made in USA

Good	Excellent	Mint
$125	**$175**	**$250**

Truck Sets

Construction Set #3109, by
Tonka, made in USA

Good	Excellent	Mint
$300	**$400**	**$500**

Semi Trailers Set, by
Ralstoy, made in USA

Set with Box- **$150**

Truck Sets

Road Builder Set #B210,
by Tonka, made in USA

Mint Boxed Set- **$3500**

Paving Dept. Set #B218,
by Tonka, made in USA

Complete Set- **$1400**

Military Vehicles (Jeeps and Automobiles)

King Jeep, 7 1/2", friction powered, by S, made in Japan

Good	Excellent	Mint
$60	$100	$140

Daring Dog Jeep, 5", friction powered, made in Japan

Good	Excellent	Mint
$45	$65	$85

Army Jeep, 10 1/2", by Clover, made in Korea

Good	Excellent	Mint
$35	$60	$100

Military Vehicles (Jeeps and Automobiles)

Army Jeep, 6 5/8", friction powered, by Yone, made in Japan

Good	Excellent	Mint
$40	**$65**	**$100**

Command Jeep, 8 1/4", friction powered, by Daiya, made in Japan

Good	Excellent	Mint
$40	**$60**	**$85**

'63 Ford Navy Car, 8", friction powered, made in Japan

Good	Excellent	Mint
$40	**$60**	**$80**

Military Vehicles (Jeeps and Automobiles)

Air-Defense Jeep, 8", friction
powered, by FN, made in Japan

Good	Excellent	Mint
$60	**$80**	**$110**

Sunbeam Jeep, 10 1/2", battery
operated, made in Japan

Good	Excellent	Mint
$90	**$150**	**$225**

Land Rover, 7 1/2", friction
powered, by Bandai, made in
Japan

Good	Excellent	Mint
$110	**$165**	**$190**

Military Vehicles (Jeeps and Automobiles)

Military Police Car, 8 1/2", battery operated, by Linemar, made in Japan

Good	Excellent	Mint
$60	$80	$110

US Air Force Jeep, 6 7/8", friction powered, made in Japan

Good	Excellent	Mint
$30	$50	$70

Anti-Aircraft Jeep, 9 1/2", battery operated, made in Japan

Good	Excellent	Mint
$50	$85	$110

Military Vehicles (Tanks)

Thunderbolt Cap Firing Tank, 6", friction powered, by Frankonia, made in Japan

Good	Excellent	Mint
$40	$65	$100

M-4 Combat Tank, 11 1/2", battery operated, by Taiyo, made in Japan

Good	Excellent	Mint
$60	$85	$125

Army Duck, 8 3/4", friction powered, made in Japan

Good	Excellent	Mint
$30	$60	$85

Military Vehicles (Tanks)

M-58 Tank, 8", friction
powered, made in Japan

Good	Excellent	Mint
$40	$60	$80

Sparkling Tank #5, 4", wind-up,
by Marx, made in USA

Good	Excellent	Mint
$30	$50	$75

Sparkling Tank, 6 1/8", friction
powered, by SY, made in Japan

Good	Excellent	Mint
$40	$65	$100

Military Vehicles (Tanks)

Tank M-15, 6", friction powered, by Daiya, made in Japan

Good	Excellent	Mint
$15	$30	$50

M-48 Army Tank, 8 1/2", battery operated, by TN, made in Japan

Good	Excellent	Mint
$40	$60	$80

Army Tank, 5 1/2", wind-up, by GAMA, made in Germany

Good	Excellent	Mint
$100	$150	$250

Military Vehicles (Tanks)

Tank, 9 1/2", wind-up, by Marx, made in Japan

Good	Excellent	Mint
$85	$110	$150

Army Tank, 10", wind-up, by Marx, made in USA

Good	Excellent	Mint
$65	$100	$135

Tank, 5 1/4", wind-up, by Marx, made in USA

Good	Excellent	Mint
$65	$85	$110

Military Vehicles (Tanks)

Tank, 10", wind-up, by Marx, made in USA

Good	Excellent	Mint
$80	$110	$150

Turnover Tank, 8", wind-up, by Marx, made in USA

Good	Excellent	Mint
$75	$100	$135

Tank, 10", wind-up, by Marx, made in USA

Good	Excellent	Mint
$45	$75	$100

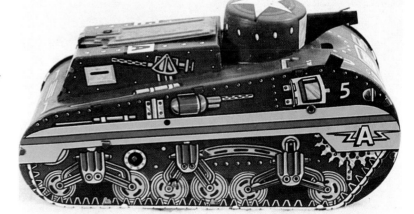

Military Vehicles (Large Vehicles and Trucks)

Chevy Rocket Launcher Truck, 11 1/2", by Y, made in Japan

Good	Excellent	Mint
$300	$400	$500

Army Plane Transport, 12 1/2", friction powered, by Bandai, made in Japan

Good	Excellent	Mint
$80	$160	$200

Pom Pom Tank, 12 1/2", battery operated, by SE, made in Japan

Good	Excellent	Mint
$60	$85	$120

Military Vehicles (Large Vehicles and Trucks)

GMC US Army Rocket
Carrier, 10", friction powered,
by Y, made in Japan

Good	Excellent	Mint
$150	**$250**	**$350**

Air Force Searchlight Truck,
17 1/4", friction and battery
powered, by Marx, made in
USA

Good	Excellent	Mint
$100	**$200**	**$275**

Sonny Army Cannon Truck,
24", pressed steel, made in USA

Good	Excellent	Mint
$900	**$1400**	-

Military Vehicles (Large Vehicles and Trucks)

Military Carrier, 21 1/2",
made in Japan

Good	Excellent	Mint
$175	**$250**	**$375**

Army Truck, 23", battery
operated, by Nylint

Good	Excellent	Mint
$80	**$125**	**$175**

Searchlight Truck, 9 1/2",
pressed steel, made in USA

Good	Excellent	Mint
$125	**$200**	**$250**

US Army Truck, 4 1/2", friction
powered, by Linemar, made in
Japan

Good	Excellent	Mint
$45	**$70**	**$95**

Military Vehicles (Large Vehicles and Trucks)

Mobile Radar Cannon Unit, 8 1/2", friction powered, by TN, made in Japan

Good	Excellent	Mint
$80	$110	$165

Army Ambulance, 27 1/2", pressed steel, by Keystone, made in USA

Good	Excellent	Mint
$1000	$1500	-

Half-Track with Cannon, 13 1/2", by Buddy L, made in USA

Good	Excellent	Mint
$80	$110	$165

US Army Tank Carrier, 10 3/4", friction powered, by Y, made in Japan

Good	Excellent	Mint
$90	$150	$225

Military Vehicles (Large Vehicles and Trucks)

Army Water Tank Truck, 9 1/2",
friction powered, by H, made
in Japan

Good	Excellent	Mint
$50	**$80**	**$100**

Army Truck, 8", friction
powered, made in Japan

Good	Excellent	Mint
$50	**$70**	**$90**

Pom Pom Truck, 12 1/2",
friction powered, by Linemar,
made in Japan

Good	Excellent	Mint
$70	**$95**	**$135**

Military Vehicles (Large Vehicles and Trucks)

Guided Missile Truck with
Red Box, 18 1/2", by Marx,
made in USA

Good	Excellent	Mint
$175	**$250**	**$300**

Guided Missile Truck with
Blue Box, 18 1/2", by Marx,
made in USA

Good	Excellent	Mint
$175	**$250**	**$300**

Army Transport Truck, 12 3/4",
friction powered, by Linemar,
made in Japan

Good	Excellent	Mint
$90	**$115**	**$155**

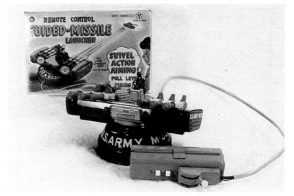

Guided Missile Launcher, 8 1/4",
battery operated, by
Yonezawa, made in Japan

Good	Excellent	Mint
$60	**$80**	**$100**

Miscellaneous Military Toys

1920 WWI Tank, 11 1/2", by Structo, made in USA

Good	Excellent	Mint
$200	**$300**	**$400**

Camouflage Motorcycle, 5 1/2", wind-up, by DRP, made in Germany

Good	Excellent	Mint
$200	**$350**	**$500**

Military Motorcycle, 5 3/4", friction powered, made in Great Britain

Good	Excellent	Mint
$150	**$210**	**$275**

Miscellaneous Military Toys

Military Vehicle Set, app. 5"
vehicles, friction powered,
by NGS, made in Japan

Set with Box- **$360**

'60's G.I. Joe with Accessories, by Hasbro, made in
USA

Good	Excellent	Mint
$100	**$200**	**$300**

Periscope Firing Range, 8 1/2",
by Cragstan, made in Japan

Good	Excellent	Mint
$75	**$100**	**$135**

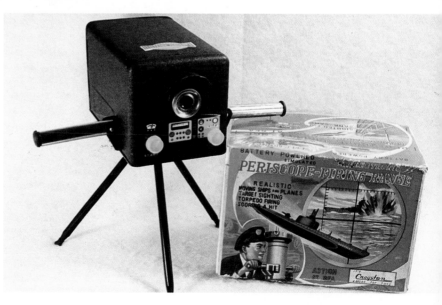

Miscellaneous Military Toys

Aircraft Carrier, 9 1/2",
friction powered, by NS,
made in Japan

Good	Excellent	Mint
$75	$135	$185

U.S. Army Fighting L.S.T.,
18", battery operated, by
Marx, made in USA

Good	Excellent	Mint
$300	$425	$600

Aircraft Carrier, 21 1/4",
battery operated, by Marx,
made in USA

Good	Excellent	Mint
$300	$450	$675

Miscellaneous Military Toys

Cap Pistol, 3 1/2", by YS,
made in Japan

Good   Excellent   Mint
$10   **$15**   **$25**

Cannon, 13 3/4", pressed steel

Good   Excellent   Mint
$30   **$70**   **$100**

Mechanical Combat Soldier,
6", wind-up, by TN, made in
Japan

Good   Excellent   Mint
$50   **$80**   **$120**

Miscellaneous Military Toys

Army Helicopter, 8", wind-up and friction powered, by Marusan, made in Japan

Good	Excellent	Mint
$60	**$85**	**$125**

U.S. Army Nike SAM-A7, 7 1/4", by S Fine Toys, made in Japan

Good	Excellent	Mint
$40	**$50**	**$65**

Helicopter, 13", friction powered, by Alps, made in Japan

Good	Excellent	Mint
$90	**$140**	**$175**

Aircraft

Operation: Airlift Airport Tower, 6", wind-up, by Automatic Toy Co., made in USA

Good	Excellent	Mint
$150	$200	$250

Training Plane, 3 1/2", made in China

Good	Excellent	Mint
$5	$10	$20

Airplane, 9 1/2" wingspan, pressed steel, by Wyandotte, made in USA

Good	Excellent	Mint
$100	$150	$175

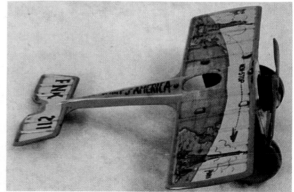

Spirit of America Airplane, 6", wind-up, made in USA

Good	Excellent	Mint
$100	$150	$225

Aircraft

Fleet Flyer #26, 9", by
Sunny Andy, made in USA

Good	Excellent	Mint
$85	$120	$180

Single Engine Airplane, 20"
wingspan, by Steelcraft,
made in USA

Good	Excellent	Mint
$475	$750	-

Air-E-Go-Round, 5" base, lever action,
by Reeves Mfg. Co., made in USA

Good	Excellent	Mint
$220	$375	$475

P-47 Cap Firing Fighter Plane, 5 3/4",
by Frankonia, made in Japan

Good	Excellent	Mint
$35	$60	$80

Aircraft

US Mail Tri-Motor Plane, 26"
wingspan, by Steelcraft, made in
USA

Good	Excellent	Mint
$675	**$1100**	-

Single Engine Airplane, 23" wingspan, by Steelcraft, made in USA

Good	Excellent	Mint
$300	**$550**	-

Lockheed Sirius, 23" wingspan, by Steelcraft, made in
USA

Good	Excellent	Mint
$800	**$1500**	-

Lockheed Sirius, 23" wingspan,
by Steelcraft, made in USA

Good	Excellent	Mint
$800	**$1500**	-

Boats and Boat Motors

Runner-Boat and Motor, 11", remote control, battery operated, made in Japan

Good Excellent Mint
$40 $80 $100

Lang Craft Boat and Motor, 15 1/4", battery operated, made in Japan

Good Excellent Mint
$50 $90 $115

Champion Racing Boat 2-J, 12", battery operated, made in Japan

Good Excellent Mint
$100 $150 $200

Boats and Boat Motors

Express Cruiser, 9", wind-up,
by Bandai, made in Japan

Good	Excellent	Mint
$50	$75	$100

Dragon Speed Boat, 18",
battery operated

Good	Excellent	Mint
$120	$250	$500

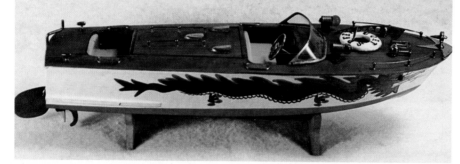

Speed Boat and Motor, 8 1/8",
by Haji, made in Japan

Good	Excellent	Mint
$25	$50	$75

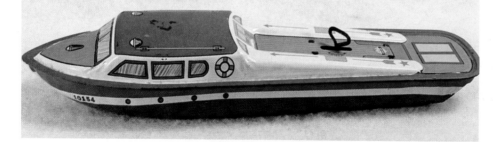

Boat, 14 1/2", wind-up, by
Ohio Art, made in USA

Good	Excellent	Mint
$50	$70	$90

Swift Boat #15, 4 1/4",
friction powered, by K,
made in Japan

Good	Excellent	Mint
$20	$40	$60

Boats and Boat Motors

Phillips 66 Power Yacht and Marina Accessory Kit, 19", by Republic Tool and Die, made in USA

Mint with Box- **$175**

Boat with Evinrude Motor, 18", boat made in USA, motor made in Japan

Good	Excellent	Mint
$180	**$250**	**$325**

Boat with Scott Atwater Motor, 18", boat made in USA, motor made in Japan

Good	Excellent	Mint
$180	**$250**	**$325**

Thunder Boat, 10", remote control, made in Japan

Good	Excellent	Mint
$80	**$100**	**$135**

Boats and Boat Motors

Fleetline Marlin Speedboat
with Evinrude Motor, 16 1/2",
battery operated, by Fleetline,
made in USA

Good	Excellent	Mint
$155	**$200**	**$275**

Ferry Boat with Two Cars,
10 3/4", friction powered,
by Linemar, made in Japan

Good	Excellent	Mint
$100	**$150**	**$175**

Evinrude Outboard Engines,
5 1/2" tall, battery operated,
made in Japan

Good	Excellent	Mint
$100	**$150**	**$200**

Boats and Boat Motors

Johnson Outboard Engines 25 and 30, 5 1/2" tall, battery operated, made in Japan

Good	Excellent	Mint
$90	$140	$185

Outboard Engine, 5" tall, battery operated, made in Japan

Good	Excellent	Mint
$15	$25	$50

Outboard Speed Engine, 5 1/2" tall, battery operated, made in Japan

Good	Excellent	Mint
$20	$35	$75

Boats and Boat Motors

Outboard Engine, 5 1/2",
battery operated

Good	Excellent	Mint
$40	**$70**	**$100**

Outboard Engine, 5 3/4" tall, gas
powered, by Atwood, made in USA

Good	Excellent	Mint
$80	**$140**	**$175**

Buccaneer 25 Outboard
Engine, 5 1/2", battery
operated, made in Japan

Good	Excellent	Mint
$75	**$120**	**$160**

Boats and Boat Motors

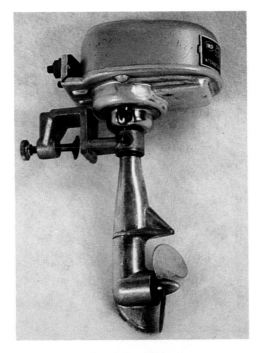

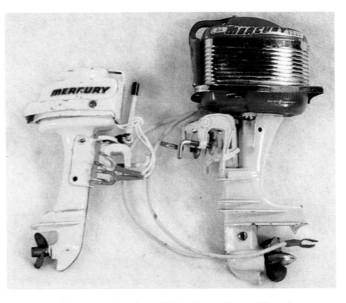

Outboard Engine, 4", battery operated, by K&O, made in Japan

Good	Excellent	Mint
$25	$50	$75

Mercury Outboard Engines, 4" and 5 1/4" tall, battery operated, made in Japan

4" Engine

Good	Excellent	Mint
$45	$70	$100

5 1/4" Engine

Good	Excellent	Mint
$100	$150	$200

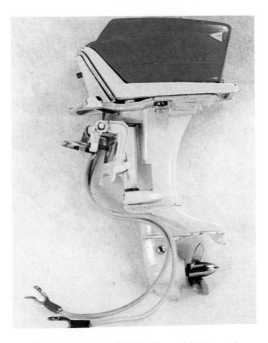

Scott-Atwater 30 Outboard Motor, 5 1/4" tall, battery operated, made in Japan

Good	Excellent	Mint
$65	$110	$155

Outboard Engines, 5 3/4" tall, gas powered, by Atwood, made in USA

Good	Excellent	Mint
$80	$140	$175

Boats and Boat Motors

Neptune Outboard Engines, 4" tall, battery operated, by Marusan, made in Japan

Mint in Package- $55

Sea Fury Outboard Engine, 4", gas powered, by Allyn, made in USA

Good	Excellent	Mint
$100	$150	$200

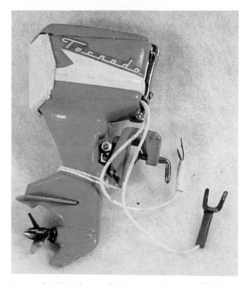

Tornado Outboard Motor, 4 3/4" tall, battery operated, by Imp, made in Japan

Good	Excellent	Mint
$40	$60	$80

Johnson Outboard Motors, (left to right): 4 3/4"; 4 1/2"; 3 1/2"; 3 1/2"; battery operated, made in Japan

4 3/4" and 4 1/2"

Good	Excellent	Mint
$75	$100	$125

3 1/2" and 3 1/2"

Good	Excellent	Mint
$30	$45	$70

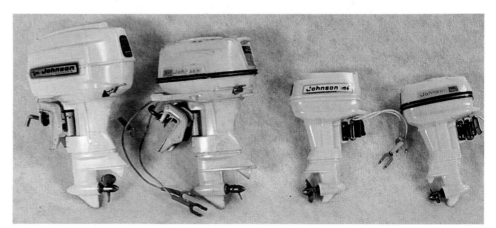

Carts and Buggies

New Milk Wagon and Horse,
10 1/2", wind-up, by Marx,
made in USA

Good	Excellent	Mint
$150	**$250**	**$325**

Baby Carriage, 9"

Good	Excellent	Mint
$35	**$60**	**$100**

Baby Carriage, 5 1/4", by Ges
Gesch, made in Germany

Good	Excellent	Mint
$60	**$80**	**$125**

Carts and Buggies

Covered Wagon, 7 3/4", by
Alps, made in Japan

Good   Excellent   Mint
$50   **$80**   **$125**

Jenny the Balking Mule,
10", wind-up, by Strauss,
made in USA

Good   Excellent   Mint
$100   **$175**   **$250**

Wildfire Trotter, 8 1/2", wind-up,
by Strauss, made in USA

Good   Excellent   Mint
$175   **$250**   **$350**

Hee Haw Mule and Cart, 10 1/2",
wind-up, by Marx, made in USA

Good   Excellent   Mint
$90   **$140**   **$200**

Carts and Buggies

The Powerful Katrinka, 7",
wind-up, by Fontaine Fox 1923,
made in Germany

Good	Excellent	Mint
$1300	$2100	$2700

Horse and Milk Wagon, 12 1/4",
pulltoy, made in USA

Good	Excellent	Mint
$120	$185	$260

Duo (Rooster and Rabbit), 7 1/2",
wind-up, by Lehmann,
made in Germany

Good	Excellent	Mint
$400	$800	$1000

Carts and Buggies

Dare Devil, 7", by Lehmann,
made in Germany

Good	Excellent	Mint
$400	$530	$650

Toytown Dairy Wagon,
10", wind-up, by Marx,
made in USA

Good	Excellent	Mint
$130	$180	$240

Toyland's Farm Products,
10 1/2", wind-up, by Marx,
made in USA

Good	Excellent	Mint
$150	$200	$260

Bicycles, Tricycles, and Go-Carts

Ice Cream Delivery Cycle, 6 1/4",
wind-up, by KO, made in Japan

Good	Excellent	Mint
$175	**$300**	**$400**

Three Wheel Mazda, 8 1/2",
friction powered, by Bandai,
made in Japan

Good	Excellent	Mint
$150	**$300**	**$375**

Ice Cream Tricycle, 9", made
in Spain

Good	Excellent	Mint
$20	**$40**	**$85**

Bicycles, Tricycles, and Go-Carts

Spin Cart Spin-A-Roo, 6 1/8",
wind-up, by Alps, made in Japan

Good	Excellent	Mint
$75	$150	$275

Ice Cream Delivery, 6 1/2",
wind-up, by Courtland,
made in USA

Good	Excellent	Mint
$150	$200	$250

Go Karting, 6", plastic, battery
operated, by Korris Products
Inc., made in USA

Mint in Package- **$75**

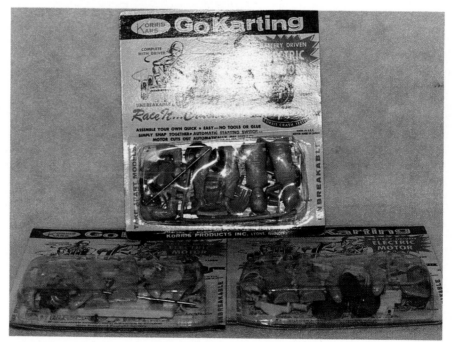

Bicycles, Tricycles, and Go-Carts

Cycling Pet, 4 1/2", wind-up, by K, made in Japan

Good	Excellent	Mint
$40	$65	$90

Bunny Tricycle, 8 1/2", wind-up, prewar, made in Japan

Good	Excellent	Mint
$275	$400	$550

Dog on Three Wheels, 7", pull toy, by Chein, made in USA

Good	Excellent	Mint
$300	$500	$800

Bicycles, Tricycles, and Go-Carts

Girl Riding Tricycle, 4", by MTU, made in Korea

Good   Excellent   Mint
$10 $20 $35

Ice Cream Vender Cart, 4", wind-up, made in China

Good   Excellent   Mint
-        $10 $15

Ice Cream Vender, 10", battery operated, made in Japan

Good   Excellent   Mint
$300 $550 $700

Motorcycles

Racing Motorcycle, 8", friction powered, by ATC, made in Japan

Good	Excellent	Mint
$90	**$125**	**$160**

Smitty Motorcycle with Sidecar, 3", by Tootsietoy, made in USA

Good	Excellent	Mint
$180	**$250**	**$300**

Echo Motorcycle, 8 3/4", wind-up, by Lehmann, made in Germany

Good	Excellent	Mint
$900	**$1450**	**$1900**

Motorcycles

Motorcycle with Sidecar, 12", by Tippco, made in Germany

Good	Excellent	Mint
$3800	$5800	$8000

Motorcycle with Sidecar, 4", wind-up, by SFA, made in France

Good	Excellent	Mint
$90	$150	$200

Speed Boy Delivery, 10", wind-up, by Marx, made in USA

Good	Excellent	Mint
$200	$400	$675

Motorcycles

Motorcycles, 3 3/4"

Good	Excellent	Mint
$100	$140	$175

Hubley Harley Cycles,
8 1/2", custom by
Lennie, made in USA

Each- $300

Racing Motorcycle, 10",
battery operated, by Daiya,
made in Japan

Good	Excellent	Mint
$65	$90	$130

Trains and Trolleys

Honeymoon Express, 9 1/4",
wind-up, by Marx, made in USA

Good	Excellent	Mint
$100	**$150**	**$200**

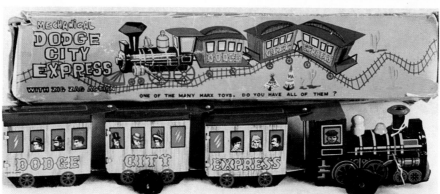

Dodge City Express, 12 3/4",
wind-up, by Marx Toys, made
in Japan

Good	Excellent	Mint
$30	**$50**	**$75**

Choo Choo Train W-99, 22",
made in West Germany

Good	Excellent	Mint
$30	**$50**	**$75**

Trains and Trolleys

Western Express, 11", wind-up, by TT, made in Japan

Good	Excellent	Mint
$15	**$30**	**$50**

New York Express, 9 1/4", wind-up, by Marx, made in USA

Good	Excellent	Mint
$700	**$900**	**$1200**

Trolley, 7 3/4", battery operated, by Modern Toys, made in Japan

Good	Excellent	Mint
$50	**$70**	**$90**

Trains and Trolleys

Train, 9", pull toy, by Metal Masters, made in USA

Good	Excellent	Mint
$40	$80	$100

Train Engine and Coal Car, 7 1/2", by K, made in Japan

Good	Excellent	Mint
$60	$100	$140

Animal Express, 9 1/4", friction powered, by TT, made in Japan

Good	Excellent	Mint
$25	$40	$55

Trains and Trolleys

Cocoa Puffs Train, 12 3/4",
wind-up, by Linemar,
made in Japan

Good	Excellent	Mint
$100	$150	$185

Crazy Express, 12 3/4",
wind-up, by Marx, made
in USA

Good	Excellent	Mint
$15	$25	$35

New York World's Fair
Greyhound Tram, 12", cast
iron, made in USA

Good	Excellent	Mint
$225	$350	$475

Coal Train, 16 3/4", friction
powered, by Sanahin, made
in Japan

Good	Excellent	Mint
$10	$20	$35

GMC Street Car, 6", by
General Models Corp.,
made in USA

Good	Excellent	Mint
$25	$40	$60

Trains and Trolleys

Hobo Train Car, 7 3/4", wind-up, by Unique Art Mfg. Co., made in USA

Good	Excellent	Mint
$250	**$400**	**$500**

Magic Tunnel, 9 1/4", wind-up, made in Japan

Good	Excellent	Mint
$65	**$90**	**$120**

New York World's Fair Greyhound Glide-A-Ride, 9", by Lowell Toy Mfg., made in USA

Good	Excellent	Mint
$125	**$200**	**$250**

Riding Toys

Dump Truck, 24 1/2", pressed steel, by Keystone, made in USA

Good	Excellent	Mint
$250	**$400**	-

Water Tower Truck, 30", pressed steel, by Keystone, made in USA

Good	Excellent	Mint
$800	**$1200**	-

Greyhound Bus with Hinged Opening Roof, 31", pressed steel, by Keystone, made in USA

Good	Excellent	Mint
$1800	**$3500**	-

Riding Toys

Dump Truck, 22 1/2", pressed steel, by Richard Toys, made in Canada

Good	Excellent	Mint
$150	$250	$350

Steam Shovel Truck, 30", pressed steel, by Richard Toys, made in Canada

Good	Excellent	Mint
$175	$300	$400

7-Up Truck, 26", pressed steel, by Richard Toys, made in Canada

Good	Excellent	Mint
$225	$400	$500

Circus Trucks

Merry-Go-Round Truck, 11",
battery operated, by TN,
made in Japan

Good	Excellent	Mint
$200	$400	$500

Merry-Go-Round Trucks,
8 1/4", friction powered, by
TN, made in Japan

Good	Excellent	Mint
$90	$160	$190

Singing Circus, 10 3/4",
battery operated, by TOM,
made in Japan

Good	Excellent	Mint
$45	$80	$140

Circus Trucks

Merry Ballblower Circus Truck, 4 1/2",
wind-up, by KO, made in Japan

Good	Excellent	Mint
$65	$100	$150

Merry-Go-Round Truck, 8 1/2",
remote control, by TN, made in
Japan

Good	Excellent	Mint
$75	$110	$165

Ferris Wheel, 8 1/2", friction
powered, by TN, made in Japan

Good	Excellent	Mint
$90	$140	$185

American Circus, 20", by K,
made in Japan

Good	Excellent	Mint
$80	$120	$200

Circus Trucks

Carousel Truck, 7 1/2",
friction powered, by Marx,
made in Japan

Good	Excellent	Mint
$80	$120	$160

World Circus, 9", friction
powered, by M, made in
Japan

Good	Excellent	Mint
$100	$150	$200

Menagerie Truck, 10", by Y,
made in Japan

Good	Excellent	Mint
$80	$110	$150

World Circus Truck, 10",
friction powered, by TN,
made in Japan

Good	Excellent	Mint
$90	$125	$165

Clowns and Circus Toys

Circus Plane, 3 1/4", wind-up,
by Yone, made in Japan

Good	Excellent	Mint
$40	**$100**	**$125**

Circus Wagon and Horse, 7 3/4",
wind-up, by SL, made in Hong
Kong

Good	Excellent	Mint
$5	**$10**	**$25**

Comic Circus Motorcycle, 6",
wind-up, made in Japan

Good	Excellent	Mint
$100	**$150**	**$200**

Clowns and Circus Toys

Toe Joe, 9 1/4", by Ohio Art Co., made in USA

Good	Excellent	Mint
$50	$100	$150

Clown Calliope, 11", plays music, by Nosco Plastic, made in USA

Good	Excellent	Mint
$100	$200	$300

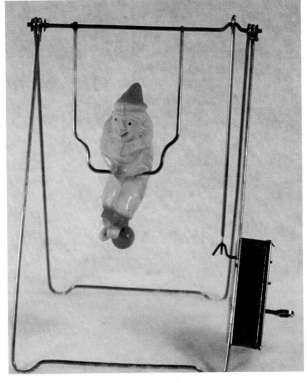

Swinging Clown, 8 1/2" tall, wind-up, made in Japan

Good	Excellent	Mint
$60	$85	$140

Clowns and Circus Toys

Krazy Kar, 8", wind-up, by Strauss, made in USA

Good	Excellent	Mint
$165	**$250**	**$350**

Circus Car, 5 1/2", wind-up, by M, made in Japan

Good	Excellent	Mint
$120	**$170**	**$200**

Loop The Loop Clown, 6 1/2", wind-up, by TN, made in Japan

Good	Excellent	Mint
$60	**$85**	**$110**

Flying Circus, 27", wind-up, made in USA

Good	Excellent	Mint
$500	**$900**	**$1250**

Clowns and Circus Toys

Monkey, 3", wind-up, made in US Zone Germany

Good	Excellent	Mint
$65	$110	$140

Big Top, 7 1/4", lever action, by Chein, made in USA

Good	Excellent	Mint
$40	$80	$110

Jumbo Elephant, 4 1/2", wind-up, made in US Zone Germany

Good	Excellent	Mint
$100	$150	$200

Elephant wind-up, 3 1/4", wind-up

Good	Excellent	Mint
$50	$75	$100

Clowns and Circus Toys

Circus Elephant, 5 3/4",
wind-up, by KSK, made in
Japan

Good	Excellent	Mint
$45	$90	$125

See Saw Circus, 9", by Lewco
Products, made in USA

Good	Excellent	Mint
$70	$125	$175

Clown in the Box, 5 1/2", by
Mattel, made in USA

Good	Excellent	Mint
$20	$35	$60

Clown Car, 7 1/4", wind-up,
by HNF, made in Germany

RARE

Clowns and Circus Toys

Jack in the Box, by Mattel
1971, made in USA

Good   Excellent   Mint
$10   **$25**   **$50**

Clown in the Box, 5 3/4",
by Lorraine Novelty Co.,
made in USA

Good   Excellent   Mint
$20   **$40**   **$75**

Clown, 4 3/4" tall, wind-up,
by Chein, made in USA

Good   Excellent   Mint
$70   **$110**   **$140**

Balancing Bear, 5" tall, made in Japan

Good   Excellent   Mint
$35   **$50**   **$75**

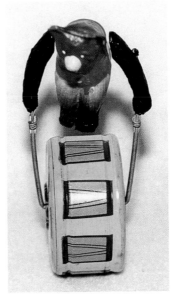

Clowns and Circus Toys

American Circus Monkeys, 6" tall, wind-up, by M, made in Japan

Good	Excellent	Mint
$125	$225	$375

Rolly Poly, 9 3/4" tall, made in Germany

Good	Excellent	Mint
$100	$175	$250

Clown with Trick Dog, 6", wind-up, by TPS, made in Japan

Good	Excellent	Mint
$90	$135	$165

Clown on High Wheel Bike, 7" tall, wind-up, by TPS, made in Japan

Good	Excellent	Mint
$140	$200	$275

Circus Train, 15", friction powered, made in Japan

Good	Excellent	Mint
$50	$75	$100

Disney and Other Cartoon Characters

Disneyland Games, box 18" x 12", by Jacmar, made in USA

Complete Set- **$150**

Snow White Top, 6 1/2", by Chein, made in USA

Good	Excellent	Mint
$40	**$75**	**$100**

Mickey Mouse Choo Choo Train, 8 1/2", pull toy, by Fisher-Price, made in USA

Good	Excellent	Mint
$90	**$140**	**$235**

Mickey Mouse Puddle Jumper, 6 1/4", pull toy, by Fisher-Price, made in USA

Good	Excellent	Mint
$80	**$130**	**$225**

Disney and Other Cartoon Characters

Disneyland Jeep, 9 3/4", by
Marx, made in Japan

Good	Excellent	Mint
$165	$200	$275

Mousketeer "Television" Record
Player, 13 1/2" x 9 1/2", by Superior
Electric Phonograph, made in USA

Complete Set- **$1500**

Casey Jr. Disneyland
Express, 12 3/4", wind-up,
by Marx, made in USA

Good	Excellent	Mint
$40	$100	$150

Elephant and Mickey
Wagon, 16", pull toy, by Toy
Kraft, made in USA

Good	Excellent	Mint
$80	$110	$160

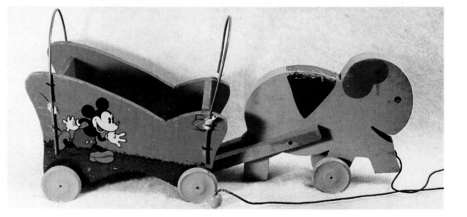

Disney and Other Cartoon Characters

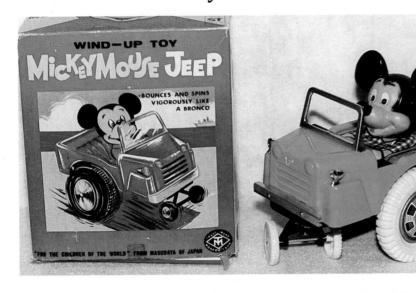

Mickey Mouse Jeep, 6", wind-up, by Modern Toys, made in Japan

Mint with Box- **$375**

National Duck Bank, 6 1/2"

Good	Excellent	Mint
$100	**$150**	**$225**

Popeye in Barrel, 7" tall, by Chein, made in USA

Good	Excellent	Mint
$400	**$650**	**$950**

Popeye Express, 9 1/2", wind-up, by Marx, made in USA

Good	Excellent	Mint
$600	**$850**	**$1200**

Disney and Other Cartoon Characters

Popeye Paddle Wagons, by
Corgi, made in Great Britain

5" Paddlewagon

Good	Excellent	Mint
$120	$200	$275

3" Paddlewagon

Good	Excellent	Mint
$45	$100	$135

Batmobile with Batboat,
11", by Corgi, made in
Great Britain

Good	Excellent	Mint
$65	$175	$300

Superman and Tank (two
views shown), 4", wind-up,
by Marx, made in USA

Good	Excellent	Mint
$200	$400	$600

Disney and Other Cartoon Characters

Mr. Magoo Car, 9", battery operated, by Hubley 1961, made in Japan

Good	Excellent	Mint
$110	$170	$250

Roy Rogers Dodge Truck and Trailer, 15 1/4", by Marx, made in USA

Good	Excellent	Mint
$120	$250	$375

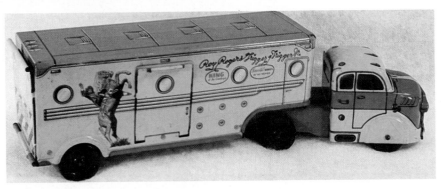

Dick Tracy Squad Car #1, 11 1/4", wind-up, by Marx, made in USA

Good	Excellent	Mint
$80	$135	$170

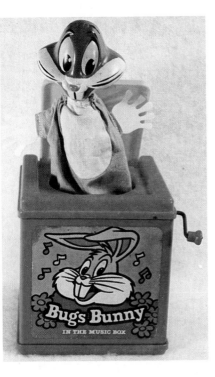

Bugs Bunny in the Box, 5 1/4", by Mattel, made in USA

Good	Excellent	Mint
$10	$30	$50

Disney and Other Cartoon Characters

Tom and Jerry Hand Car (Jerry Mouse Version), 8",
battery operated, by Modern Toys, made in Japan

Good	Excellent	Mint
$150	**$230**	**$325**

Tom and Jerry Hand Car (Tom the Cat Version), 8",
battery operated, by Modern Toys, made in Japan

Good	Excellent	Mint
$150	**$230**	**$325**

Disney and Other Cartoon Characters

Tom and Jerry in the Box, 5 1/4",
by Mattel, made in USA

Good	Excellent	Mint
$30	$55	$90

Howdy Doody Trapeze Artist, 16" tall, spring wind-up action, by Arnold, made in West Germany

Good	Excellent	Mint
$50	$90	$175

Uncle Wiggily Crazy Car, 8", wind-up, made in USA

Good	Excellent	Mint
$450	$700	$950

Popeye Train Set, 5" each, made in Hong Kong

Mint with Package- $45

293

Tin Toys

Singing Bird, 4 3/4" tall,
wind-up, by TN, made in
Japan

Good	Excellent	Mint
$30	$50	$75

Frog, 4" tall, wind-up

Good	Excellent	Mint
$25	$50	$75

See Saw, 7" tall, by Chein, made in USA

Good	Excellent	Mint
$40	$75	$125

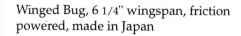

Winged Bug, 6 1/4" wingspan, friction
powered, made in Japan

Good	Excellent	Mint
$40	$60	$85

Tin Toys

Suzy Bouncing Ball, 5 1/2"
tall, wind-up, by TPS, made
in Japan

Good	Excellent	Mint
$75	$125	$150

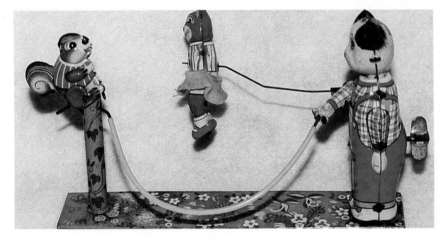

Jumping Rope, 8", wind-up,
by TPS, made in Japan

Good	Excellent	Mint
$75	$110	$175

Penguin, 4 1/4" tall, wind-
up, by Chein, made in USA

Good	Excellent	Mint
$50	$85	$135

Percy Penguin, 5", friction
powered, by TN, made in
Japan

Good	Excellent	Mint
$80	$110	$150

Tin Toys

Boxing Ring, 3 1/2", wind-up, made in Germany

Good	Excellent	Mint
$150	$265	$350

Piggy, 4 1/2", by Chein, made in USA

Good	Excellent	Mint
$70	$90	$120

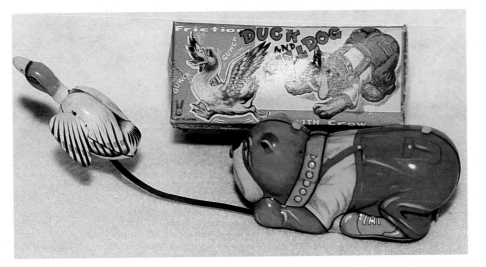

Duck and Bulldog, 8 1/4", friction powered, made in Japan

Good	Excellent	Mint
$80	$110	$140

Waiter, 6 1/2" tall, wind-up, by Yone, made in Japan

Good	Excellent	Mint
$80	$100	$150

Tin Toys

Tiger, 5 1/2", wind-up, made in Japan

Good	Excellent	Mint
$30	**$60**	**$85**

Bear, 4 3/4", wind-up, by Chein, made in USA

Good	Excellent	Mint
$55	**$80**	**$110**

Flippo Dog, 3 3/4" tall, wind-up, by Marx, made in USA

Good	Excellent	Mint
$30	**$50**	**$75**

Turkey, 4", wind-up

Good	Excellent	Mint
$40	**$65**	**$90**

Tin Toys

All Stars, 8 1/4" tall, battery
operated, by K, made in Japan

Good	Excellent	Mint
$200	$350	$450

Noise Makers, 4 3/4" each, by Kirchhof
and US Metal Mfg. Co., made in USA

Each- $15

Magic Fish, 6 1/2" big fish,
made in Japan

Good	Excellent	Mint
$35	$60	$80

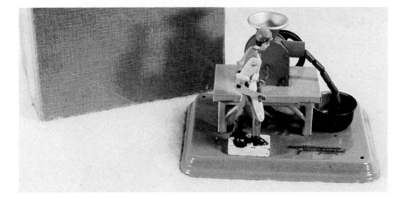

Sausage Maker, 5 1/4", by
Fleishmann, made in Germany

Good	Excellent	Mint
$65	$100	$165

Tin Toys

Mechanical Duck, 7 1/4", wind-up, by Lindstrom, made in USA

Good   Excellent   Mint
$40   **$80**   **$125**

Animal Barber, 4 3/4", wind-up, by TPS, made in Japan

Good   Excellent   Mint
$185   **$300**   **$375**

Kadi, 7", by Lehmann, made in Germany

Good   Excellent   Mint
$500   **$650**   **$950**

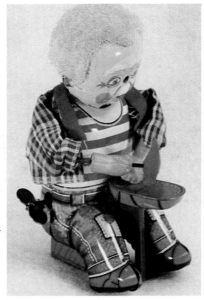

Cobbler, 6" tall, wind-up, made in Japan

Good   Excellent   Mint
$45   **$100**   **$125**

Tin Toys

Bunny Family Parade, 12 1/2",
wind-up, by TPS, made in Japan

Good	Excellent	Mint
$40	**$75**	**$100**

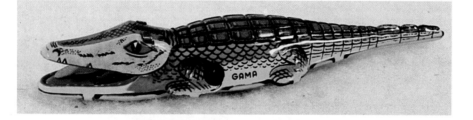

Crocodile, 6 1/2", wind-up,
by GAMA, made in US
Zone Germany

Good	Excellent	Mint
$85	**$120**	**$150**

Alligator, 8 3/4", wind-up,
made in Germany

Good	Excellent	Mint
$115	**$155**	**$225**

Golden Goose, 9 1/4", wind-
up, by Marx, made in USA

Good	Excellent	Mint
$75	**$100**	**$150**

Tin Toys

Rocking Dog with Whirling Rope, 5 3/4" tall, wind-up, by K, made in Japan

Good	Excellent	Mint
$60	$85	$125

Music Box, 5", wind-up, by Ohio Art Co., made in USA

Good	Excellent	Mint
$30	$45	$75

Jocko the Drinking Monkey, 10 1/2", battery operated, by Linemar Toys, made in Japan

Good	Excellent	Mint
$80	$120	$145

Tin Toys

Jocko the Climbing Monkey, 6 3/8",
by Linemar Toys, made in Japan

Good	Excellent	Mint
$25	$40	$65

Mattel Merry Music Box, 8",
wind-up, by Mattel, made in USA

Good	Excellent	Mint
$50	$80	$100

Mule Drinking Water, 6 3/4", made in Germany

Good	Excellent	Mint
$170	$300	$400

Indian Canoe, 9 1/2", friction
powered, made in Japan

Good	Excellent	Mint
$300	$525	$675

Tin Toys

Snapping Alligator, 12 1/4", wind-up, by Cragstan, made in Japan

Good	Excellent	Mint
$35	$60	$85

Snapping Alligator, 12 1/4", wind-up, by Cragstan, made in Japan

Good	Excellent	Mint
$35	$60	$85

Dancing Man, 8 3/4", wind-up, by S&E, made in Japan

Good	Excellent	Mint
$80	$100	$150

Steam Toy, 5", made in Germany

Good	Excellent	Mint
$50	$75	$100

Tin Toys

Cat with Ball, 3 1/2", wind-up, by Kahler, made in US Zone Germany

Good	Excellent	Mint
$30	$60	$100

Penny Toy Scale, 2 3/4", made in Germany

Good	Excellent	Mint
$90	$110	$165

Butterfly, 3 1/2", wind-up, made in Occupied Japan

Good	Excellent	Mint
$30	$40	$60

Phillips 66 Bank, 2 3/4" tall, made in USA

Good	Excellent	Mint
$20	$35	$50

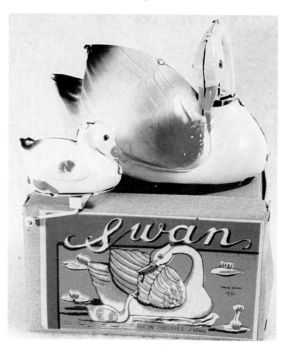

Swan, 5 1/4", wind-up, by TN, made in Japan

Good	Excellent	Mint
$50	$85	$125

Robots and Space Toys

Buck Rogers School Set
(details below)
Buck Rogers Flying Saucer,
6 1/4", made in USA

Good	Excellent	Mint
$85	$120	$155

Buck Rogers School Set, 8 1/4",
made in USA 1936

Good	Excellent	Mint
$95	$150	$175

Buck Rogers Rocketship, 12",
wind-up, by Marx, made in USA

Good	Excellent	Mint
$300	$600	$850

Robots and Space Toys

Two-Stage Rocket Launching Pad, 8 3/4" tall, battery operated, by TN, made in Japan

Good	Excellent	Mint
$65	$120	$165

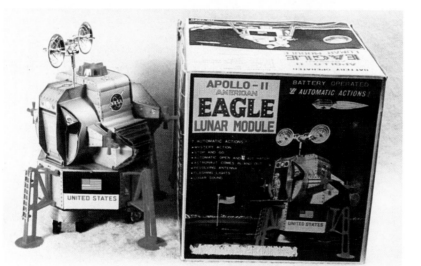

Apollo-11 American Eagle Lunar Module, 7", battery operated, by DK Co., made in Japan

Good	Excellent	Mint
$80	$115	$160

Capsule #5, 10 1/2", battery operated, by Modern Toys, made in Japan

Good	Excellent	Mint
$70	$100	$140

306

Robots and Space Toys

Capsule Mercury, 9", friction powered, by SH, made in Japan

Good	Excellent	Mint
$65	$90	$135

Universe Car, 10 1/8", battery operated, made in China

Good	Excellent	Mint
$10	$20	$30

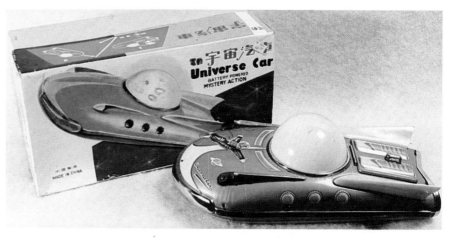

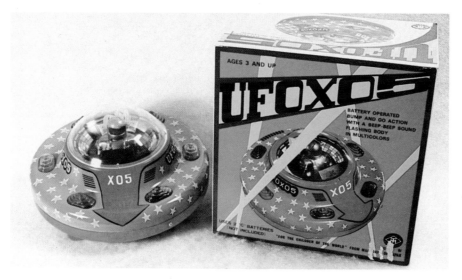

UFO #X05, 7", battery operated, by TM, made in Japan

Good	Excellent	Mint
$40	$80	$120

Robots and Space Toys

US Apollo, 10 3/4", battery
operated, by TM, made in Japan

Good	Excellent	Mint
$60	$90	$135

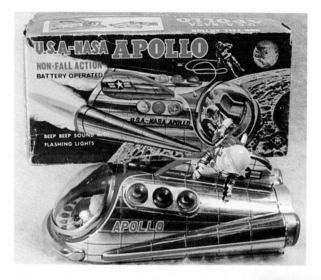

USA NASA Apollo, 9 1/2",
battery operated, by TM,
made in Japan

Good	Excellent	Mint
$80	$125	$150

Planet Patrol Puzzle, 14" x 11",
by Jaymar 1952, made in USA

Good	Excellent	Mint
$20	$40	$80

Satellite Launching Truck, 16",
friction powered, by Y, made in
Japan

Good	Excellent	Mint
$150	$250	$300

Robots and Space Toys

Delta 55 Lunar Explorer, 9 1/2",
battery operated, by Y, made in
Japan

Good	Excellent	Mint
$40	**$70**	**$90**

Captain the Robot, 5 3/4", wind-
up, by MTU, made in Korea

Good	Excellent	Mint
$40	**$60**	**$75**

Lunar Expedition, 15", wind-up, made
in West Germany

Good	Excellent	Mint
$80	**$125**	**$175**

Strato Bank, 8", diecast, made in USA

Good	Excellent	Mint
$45	**$70**	**$90**

Robots and Space Toys

Space Capsule, 9 3/4", battery operated, made in Japan

Good	Excellent	Mint
$80	**$100**	**$140**

Space Explorer Ship, 7 3/4", battery operated, by TM, made in Japan

Good	Excellent	Mint
$45	**$85**	**$125**

Flying Saucer, 7 3/4", battery operated, by KO, made in Japan

Good	Excellent	Mint
$80	**$110**	**$150**

Robots and Space Toys

Space Station, 9", battery operated, made in Japan

Good	Excellent	Mint
$100	**$200**	**$300**

Swivel-O-Matic Astronaut, 11 1/4", battery operated, by SH, made in Japan

Good	Excellent	Mint
$80	**$100**	**$125**

Space Patrol, 8 1/4", friction powered, by Cragstan, made in Japan

Good	Excellent	Mint
$800	**$1200**	**$1900**

Robots and Space Toys

Thunderbolt Special Rocket Car, 7 3/4", plastic, made in USA

Good	Excellent	Mint
$40	**$50**	**$75**

Space Capsule, 10 3/4", battery operated, by SH, made in Japan

Good	Excellent	Mint
$80	**$110**	**$140**

NASA Space Station, 11 1/2", battery operated, by SH, made in Japan

Good	Excellent	Mint
$600	**$800**	**$1000**

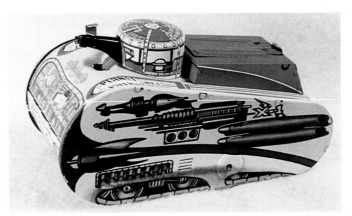

Planet Patrol, 10", wind-up, by Marx, made in USA

Good	Excellent	Mint
$180	**$250**	**$325**

Robots and Space Toys

Moon Rocket, 9 1/2", battery operated, by TM, made in Japan

Good	Excellent	Mint
$100	$150	$220

Space Station, 11", battery operated, by SH, made in Japan

Good	Excellent	Mint
$650	$1000	$1500

New Space Capsule, 9 1/4", battery operated, by SH, made in Japan

Good	Excellent	Mint
$65	$90	$135

Robots and Space Toys

Television Spaceman, 7 1/4",
wind-up, by Alps, made in
Japan

Good	Excellent	Mint
$100	**$150**	**$185**

Space Rocket, 8 3/4", friction
powered, by Automatic Toy
Co., made in USA

Good	Excellent	Mint
$100	**$200**	**$250**

Zooming Satellite, 9 3/4" box,
by GAMA, made in West
Germany

Good	Excellent	Mint
$90	**$125**	**$180**

Robots and Space Toys

Robot Operated Bulldozer, 7", battery operated, by KO, made in Japan

Good	Excellent	Mint
$300	$500	$700

Attacking Martian, 11", battery operated, by SH, made in Japan

Good	Excellent	Mint
$30	$65	$95

Mighty Robot, 5 1/2", wind-up, by N, made in Japan

Good	Excellent	Mint
$60	$80	$125

Robots and Space Toys

NASA Flying Saucer, 8", battery operated, by TM, made in Japan

Good	Excellent	Mint
$70	**$100**	**$125**

Space Dog, 7 1/2", wind-up, by KO, made in Japan

Good	Excellent	Mint
$150	**$250**	**$350**

Atomic Space Gun, 5", friction powered, made in Japan

Good	Excellent	Mint
$20	**$40**	**$50**

Burp Gun, 10 1/4", friction powered, by TN, made in Japan

Good	Excellent	Mint
$60	**$80**	**$95**

Robots and Space Toys

Space Robot Patrol, 8",
friction powered, by
Asahitoy, made in Japan

Good	Excellent	Mint
$350	$600	$800

Mercedes Robot Car, 8 1/4",
made in Japan

Good	Excellent	Mint
$500	$650	$900

Space Patrol Car, 9 5/8",
battery operated, by TN,
made in Japan

Good	Excellent	Mint
$350	$450	$600

Doll and Dollhouse Accessories

Cast Iron "Royal" Stove, 14" x
11 1/2", made in USA

Good	Excellent	Mint
$150	**$350**	**$450**

Cast Iron "Tot" Stove, 3 1/4", made in USA

Good	Excellent	Mint
$110	**$150**	**$185**

Cast Iron "Eagle" Stove, 11 1/2",
made in USA

Good	Excellent	Mint
$100	**$200**	**$300**

Doll and Dollhouse Accessories

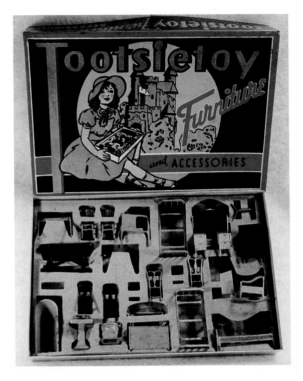

Furniture and Accessories, 15" box,
by Tootsietoy, made in USA

Good	Excellent	Mint
$150	**$250**	**$350**

Stove with Accessories, 6 1/2",
tin, made in England

Good	Excellent	Mint
$100	**$150**	**$200**

Cast Iron "Eagle" Stove, 5",
made in USA

Good	Excellent	Mint
$110	**$170**	**$220**

Doll and Dollhouse Accessories

"Venus" Stove, 8 1/2", cast iron and tin, made in USA

Good	Excellent	Mint
$125	**$200**	**$225**

Kitchen Range, made in USA

Good	Excellent	Mint
$20	**$30**	**$55**

Cast Iron "Royal" Stove, 8 1/4", made in USA

Good	Excellent	Mint
$100	**$150**	**$185**

Doll and Dollhouse Accessories

Toy Tea Set, 7 1/2" box,
made in Japan

Set with Box: **$175**

Set of Clown Dishes, made
in Japan

Good	Excellent	Mint
$75	**$125**	**$150**

Children's Tea Set with
Antique Car Prints, box 9"

Set with Box- **$275**

Carousels and Merry-Go-Rounds

Twirly Whirly Rocket Ride, 11 1/2",
battery operated, by Alps, made in Japan

Good	Excellent	Mint
$375	$600	$750

Carousel, 6", made in USA

Good	Excellent	Mint
$90	$120	$165

Merry-Go-Round, 6", made in USA

Good	Excellent	Mint
$90	$120	$165

Carousels and Merry-Go-Rounds

Mechanical Airplane Ride, 9 1/2", made in Germany

Good	Excellent	Mint
$450	**$700**	**$1000**

Music Box Carousel, 9 1/2", by Mattel, made in Canada

Good	Excellent	Mint
$55	**$90**	**$110**

Playland Merry-Go-Round, 11",
wind-up, by Chein, made in USA

Good	Excellent	Mint
$275	**$400**	**$500**

Road Race Top, 7", by Chein, made in USA

Good	Excellent	Mint
$35	**$75**	**$100**

Carousels and Merry-Go-Rounds

Mechanical Musical Carousel,
7 5/8", made in USA

Good	Excellent	Mint
$100	$140	$175

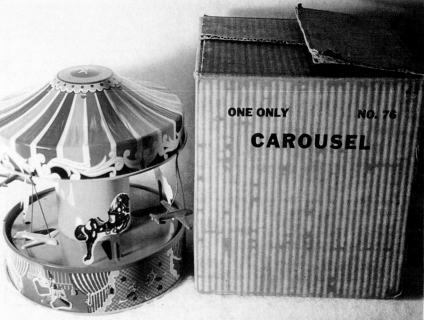

Kiddy-Go-Round (toy and box depicted); 12", wind-up, made in USA

Good	Excellent	Mint
$110	$220	$300

Carousels and Merry-Go-Rounds

Merry-Go-Round, 6 3/4" base,
wind-up, made in Germany

Good   Excellent   Mint
$800   **$1200**   **$1650**

Monkey Ferris Wheel, 8 1/2" tall,
wind-up, made in Germany

Good   Excellent   Mint
$300   **$500**   **$750**

Merry-Go-Round, 11", lever action,
by Wolverine, made in USA

Good   Excellent   Mint
$200   **$300**   **$400**

Christmas Toys

"Merry Christmas" Helicopter, 6", wind-up, made in Japan

Good	Excellent	Mint
$40	**$70**	**$85**

Santa Music Figure, 11 1/2" tall, made in Japan

Good	Excellent	Mint
$95	**$140**	**$190**

Santa's Arrival, 3 1/2", wind-up, by Alps, made in Japan

Good	Excellent	Mint
$40	**$60**	**$80**

Christmas Toys

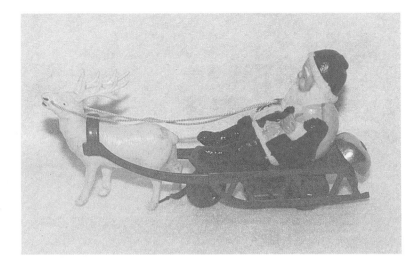

Santa on Reindeer Sleigh, 8 1/4",
tin and celluloid, wind-up, made
in Occupied Japan

Good	Excellent	Mint
$80	**$100**	**$140**

Santa on Top of the World, 15" tall,
battery operated, made in Japan

Good	Excellent	Mint
$200	**$300**	**$400**

Santa on Reindeer Sled, 17 1/4", battery
operated, by Modern Toys, made in Japan

Good	Excellent	Mint
$200	**$350**	**$465**

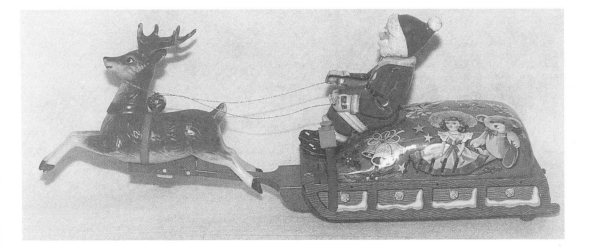

Christmas Toys

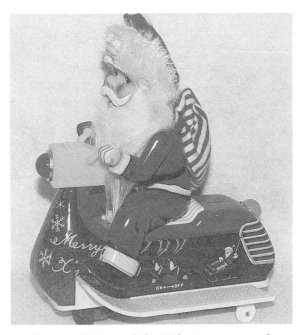

Santa on Snowmobile, 8", battery operated, by Modern Toys, made in Japan

Good	Excellent	Mint
$50	$110	$165

Santa with Sack of Toys, 9", wind-up, made in Japan

Good	Excellent	Mint
$70	$90	$125

Santa Ringing Bell, 10" tall, wind-up, made in Japan

Good	Excellent	Mint
$40	$60	$100

Santa's Car, 11", battery operated, by Roc, made in Taiwan

Good	Excellent	Mint
$35	$50	$75

Christmas Toys

Santa with Balloons, 7" tall, wind-up, made in Japan

Good	Excellent	Mint
$65	**$90**	**$125**

Santa with Bell, 10" tall, battery operated, made in Japan

Good	Excellent	Mint
$25	**$50**	**$75**

Santa on Roof, 11" tall, by HTC, made in Japan

Good	Excellent	Mint
$50	**$85**	**$110**

Santa on Roof, 8" tall, battery operated, made in Japan

Good	Excellent	Mint
$55	**$85**	**$110**

329

Games and Puzzles

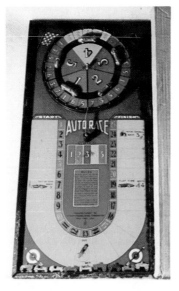

Touring Card Game, 5 1/2", by Parker Bros.

Good	Excellent	Mint
$25	**$40**	**$65**

Auto Race Game, 21 3/4", by
Gotham, made in USA

Good	Excellent	Mint
$100	**$165**	**$300**

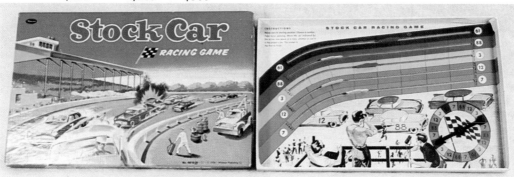

Stock Car Racing Game, 11", by
Whitman Publishing Co., made
in USA

Good	Excellent	Mint
$20	**$35**	**$50**

Automatic Racing Game, 5 3/4",
2 3/8" cars, made in Japan

Good	Excellent	Mint
$120	**$175**	**$250**

Games and Puzzles

Motor Race Game, 16 1/2", by
Wolverine, made in USA

Good	Excellent	Mint
$110	$155	$185

Famous Racing Cars Puzzle,
10" box, made in England

Complete with Box- **$125**

Tiddledy Winks, 8 1/4", by
Milton Bradley, made in
USA

Good	Excellent	Mint
$5	$10	$20

Black Memorabilia

Red Cap Porter, 8 1/2", wind-up, by Marx, made in USA

Good	Excellent	Mint
$400	**$750**	**$900**

Charleston Trio, 5", wind-up, by Marx, made in USA

Good	Excellent	Mint
$500	**$800**	**$1000**

Black Dancer, 11", wind-up, made in Japan

Good	Excellent	Mint
$235	**$375**	**$475**

Black Memorabilia

Black Waiter on Skates, 8" tall,
wind-up, made in Japan

Good   Excellent   Mint
$170   **$265**   **$350**

Dapper Dan Jigger, 10 1/4", wind-up,
by Marx, made in USA

Good   Excellent   Mint
$550   **$800**   **$1000**

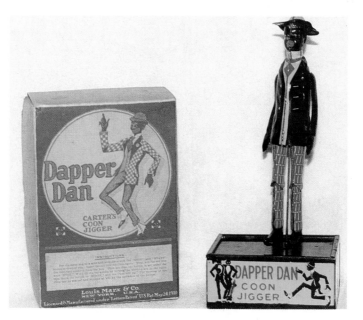

Panorama Display Sets

Roller Coaster #275, 19 1/2",
wind-up, by Chein, made in
USA

Good	Excellent	Mint
$175	**$300**	**$375**

George Washington Bridge, 25", wind-up bus, made in USA 1936

Good	Excellent	Mint
$350	**$700**	**$1200**

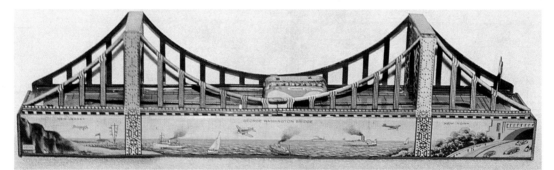

The Big Parade, 24", wind-up, by Marx, made in USA

Good	Excellent	Mint
$500	**$950**	**$1300**

Panorama Display Sets

Lincoln Tunnel, 24", wind-up, by Unique Art, made in USA

Good	Excellent	Mint
$150	**$200**	**$300**

The Big Parade, 24", wind-up, by Marx, made in USA

Good	Excellent	Mint
$400	**$800**	**$975**

Camping Set with Two Cars, 29", by Technofix, made in Germany

Good	Excellent	Mint
$100	**$145**	**$185**

Panorama Display Sets

Highway Drive, 16", battery operated, by TN, made in Japan

Good	Excellent	Mint
$60	$125	$150

ABTOTPACCA Bus Lines, 9 3/4", wind-up, made in Russia

Good	Excellent	Mint
$15	$20	$35

Streamline Speedway, 22 1/2", 4" cars, wind-up, by Marx, made in USA

Good	Excellent	Mint
$110	$140	$175

Panorama Display Sets

Speedway, 14", wind-up, made in USA

Good	Excellent	Mint
$250	**$350**	**$500**

Caterpillar Bulldozer, 15 1/4", mechanical, by TPS, made in Japan

Good	Excellent	Mint
$60	**$80**	**$95**

Miscellaneous Cast Iron Toys

Bucking Goats Penny Toy, 4 3/4",
mechanical, made in Germany

Good	Excellent	Mint
$250	**$400**	**$600**

Toledo Scale, 4 1/2", made in USA

Good	Excellent	Mint
$100	**$165**	**$250**

Boy on Sled, 9", friction
powered, made in Germany

Good	Excellent	Mint
$100	**$300**	**$400**

Miscellaneous Cast Iron Toys

Wonder Cement Mixer, 3 1/2",
made in USA

Good	Excellent	Mint
$90	**$160**	**$275**

Jaeger Cement Mixer, 9 1/2",
made in USA

Good	Excellent	Mint
$600	**$1000**	**$1500**

Ice Cream Maker Bank, 4",
made in USA

Good	Excellent	Mint
$175	**$320**	**$500**

Miscellaneous Wooden Toys

Cottontail, 12", pull toy, by
Fisher-Price, made in USA

Good	Excellent	Mint
$100	**$150**	**$200**

Sight Seeing Bus, 15", made
in USA

Good	Excellent	Mint
$200	**$350**	**$500**

Teddy Zilo, 9", pull toy, by
Fisher-Price, made in USA

Good	Excellent	Mint
$45	**$100**	**$150**

Miscellaneous Wooden Toys

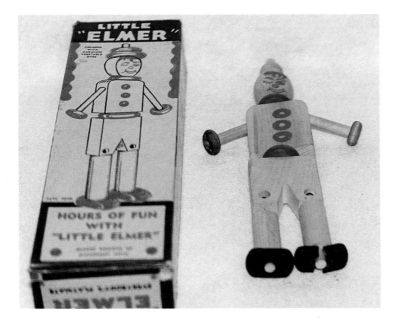

Little Elmer, 12" box, by Little
Elmer Toy Co., made in USA

Good	Excellent	Mint
$20	**$40**	**$60**

Horse and Jockey, 7 1/4", pull toy,
by Hustler Toys, made in USA

Good	Excellent	Mint
$45	**$80**	**$100**

Zoo Apart, 10 1/4", pull toy, by
Strombecker, made in USA

Good	Excellent	Mint
$35	**$60**	**$85**

Miscellaneous Toys

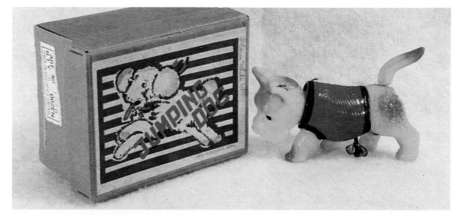

Jumping Dog, 4 3/4", celluloid, wind-up, made in Occupied Japan

Good	Excellent	Mint
$20	$35	$45

Balloon Blowing Monkey, 11", battery operated, by Alps, made in Japan

Good	Excellent	Mint
$55	$80	$150

Walking Clock, 3 1/2", wind-up, made in Japan

Good	Excellent	Mint
$20	$30	$45

Miscellaneous Toys

Jolly Chimp, 10 1/2", battery operated, by CK, made in Japan

Good	Excellent	Mint
$45	**$75**	**$100**

Children's Flat Iron, 3 1/2", made in USA

Good	Excellent	Mint
$20	**$30**	**$50**

Royal Cub, 8", by S&E, made in Japan

Good	Excellent	Mint
$75	**$100**	**$140**

Miscellaneous Toys

Bubbling Bull, 6 5/8", battery operated, by Linemar, made in Japan

Good	Excellent	Mint
$50	**$90**	**$150**

Smoking Grandpa in Rocker, 8", battery operated, made in Japan

Good	Excellent	Mint
$75	**$100**	**$150**

Spin-A-Hoop, 9" tall, wind-up, made in Japan

Good	Excellent	Mint
$65	**$100**	**$125**

Hoop Zing Girl, 11 1/2" tall, battery operated, by Linemar, made in Japan

Good	Excellent	Mint
$60	**$90**	**$125**

Miscellaneous Toys

Farm Milk Bear, 6", wind-up, made in Japan

Good	Excellent	Mint
$65	**$85**	**$110**

Josie the Cow, 13 1/2", battery operated, by Rosko, made in Japan

Good	Excellent	Mint
$40	**$75**	**$125**

Mother Bear, 9 1/2" tall, battery operated, by Modern Toys, made in Japan

Good	Excellent	Mint
$50	**$100**	**$140**

Sleeping Bear, 9", battery operated, by Linemar, made in Japan

Good	Excellent	Mint
$90	**$120**	**$160**

Miscellaneous Toys

Little Bandit Slot Machine, 2 3/4"
tall, by E.S. Lowe Co., made in USA

Good	Excellent	Mint
$5	$10	$20

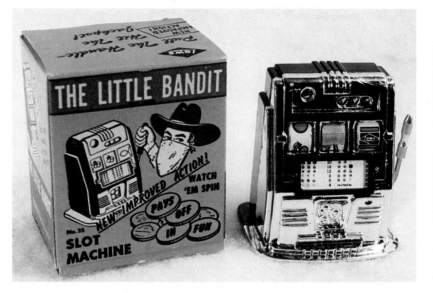

Spitfire Cap Gun, 4 3/4", by J&E
Stevens Co., made in USA

Good	Excellent	Mint
$60	$80	$120

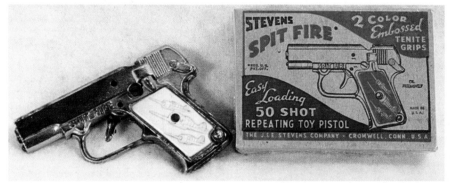

Brer-Rabbit Ring A Bunny,
10" x 8 1/4" box, by Parker
Bros., made in USA

Complete with Box- **$200**

Celluloid Bug, 3", wind-up,
made in Japan

Good	Excellent	Mint
$35	$60	$100

Miscellaneous Toys

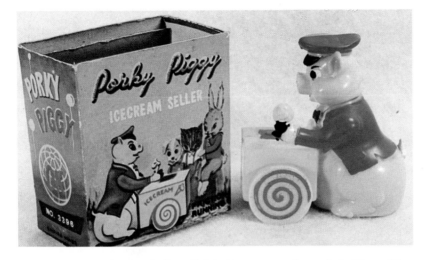

Porky Piggy Ice Cream Seller, 4", friction powered, made in Hong Kong

Good	Excellent	Mint
$30	$50	$70

Terrier, 5", wind-up, by Rock Valley Toys, made in Japan

Good	Excellent	Mint
$35	$60	$85

Baby in Walker, 4 1/2", wind-up, made in Japan

Good	Excellent	Mint
$75	$125	$185

Moby Dick, 10 1/2", plastic, wind-up, by FM Engineering Co., made in USA

Good	Excellent	Mint
$15	$20	$25

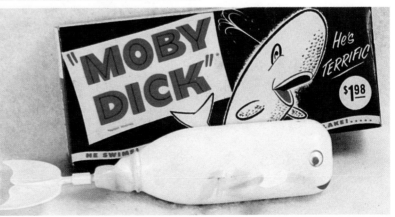

Miscellaneous Toys

Mechanical Tiger, 8 1/2", wind-up, by Marx, made in USA

Good	Excellent	Mint
$75	**$100**	**$135**

Mechanical Hula Hoop Monkey, 9 1/4", wind-up, by Plaything, made in Japan

Good	Excellent	Mint
$35	**$60**	**$85**

Mr. Bubbles, 8", plastic, by Morris, made in USA

Good	Excellent	Mint
$5	**$15**	**$35**

Flower Loving Dog, 5", wind-up, made in Japan

Good	Excellent	Mint
$20	**$45**	**$75**

Miscellaneous Toys

Washing Machine, 6" tall, battery operated, by Y, made in Japan

Good	Excellent	Mint
$30	$65	$90

Elmer Book and Elephant, made in USA

Complete- **$20**

Elephant, 7 1/4", wind-up, by CK, made in Japan

Good	Excellent	Mint
$70	$100	$125